# Born Black

# Born Black

by
## Gordon Parks

*with photographs by the author*

## J. B. Lippincott Company
Philadelphia / New York

Copyright © 1971, 1970, 1968, 1967, 1966, 1965, 1963 by
Gordon Parks
All rights reserved
10  9  8  7  6  5
Printed in the United States of America
Library of Congress Catalog Card No.: 78–146692
ISBN-0-397-00690-X

Chapter 1, "Death at San Quentin," is an adaptation of the Pro-
logue to *A Choice of Weapons* by Gordon Parks. Copyright © 1965,
1966 by Gordon Parks. Reprinted by permission of Harper & Row,
Publishers, Inc.

*For my editor, Genevieve Young*

## What I want
## What I am
## What you force me to be
## is what you are

For I am you, staring back from a mirror of poverty and despair, of revolt and freedom. Look at me and know that to destroy me is to destroy yourself. You are weary of the long hot summers. I am tired of the long hungered winters. We are not so far apart as it might seem. There is something about both of us that goes deeper than blood or black and white. It is our common search for a better life, a better world. I march now over the same ground you once marched over. I fight for the same things you still fight for. My children's needs are the same as your children's. I too am America. America is me. It gave me the only life I know—so I must share in its survival. Look at me. Listen to me. Try to understand my struggle against your racism. There is yet a chance for us to live in peace beneath these restless skies.

7

# Contents

9

# *Foreword*

In the last ten years black Americans have turned four hundred years of despair and oppression into an era of rebellion and hope. It was a turbulent decade filled with demonstrations, riots, bombings and violent death; a period in which we black people combined to mutiny against a common fate. The white symbols and images that for so long disfigured our minds and blackness are being jettisoned by that very blackness. And it was clearly revolt that had to be employed to alter this country's conduct toward us. Now we are beginning to know who we are, what we mean to America—and what America means to us.

These essays, commissioned by *Life* magazine, are

some personal observations of this time and of certain people who helped to shape it with their actions, and sometimes with their lives. I came to each story with a strong sense of involvement, finding it difficult to screen out my own memories of a scarred past. But I tried for truth, the kind that comes through looking and listening, through the careful sifting of day-to-day emotions that white America whips up in black people. My own background has enabled me, I hope, to better share the experiences of some other black people. I do not presume to speak for them. I have just offered a glimpse, however fleeting, of their world through black eyes.

GORDON PARKS

*New York City*
*October, 1970*

# Born Black

# 1. Death at San Quentin

*FEBRUARY, 1960*

*We* are standing silent in the safe quarter of this pale green gas chamber. There are twelve of us and a cocky young guard; his orders splinter my thoughts: "Don't move around—don't gesture—don't talk aloud—obey commands promptly." Now, for some unaccountable reason, the guard is motioning me down front—to within three feet of the waiting chair. From here, only a thick glass will separate me from the death we have agreed to witness. Close behind us a minister leafs his Bible for words to say at the appropriate time.

The color of the walls seems so incompatible with the occasion. Why not a somber gray or, better still, black?

The door to the cubicle is opening. The quiet is heavy, and I curse myself for accepting the warden's invitation. But it's too late for that now; the doomed man is already coming, ashen and shaking, flanked by three beefy guards. He is dressed in blue prison denim, wears gray flannel bedroom slippers and moves with a hesitant shuffle as they guide him through the door. Only the compassionate whispers of the minister stir the silence. *That the saying of Jesus might be fulfilled, which he spake, signifying what death he should die.* The prisoner observes us through tears; and, for a curious moment, his eyes seem to question our presence. He is turning slowly, using up every precious second before surrendering his body to the chair, realizing, as he must, that he will never through his own strength rise again. And I am feeling that strength ebb, as if his legs were mine suffering the disordered weakness that claimed me long ago. It is my seventeenth birthday, and I am homeless. The old streetcar conductor pokes me awake, saying we are at the end of the line. The end of the line. He stands above me, the green bills wadded together with a rubber band. My hand tightens around the switchblade in my pocket. I rise slowly looking through the ice-crusted window to see if we are alone. His back is to me as we walk toward the rear of the car. Sweat rolls from my armpits and the anxiety of evil-doing must show on my face. I press the button. The long blade pops out.

"Conductor!"

"Yes." He turns, looking calmly at the blade. I look at him, trembling now. All my mother's teaching comes hot at me.

"Conductor," I say, "would you give me a dollar for this knife? I'm hungry and I don't have a place to stay."

The old man watches me for a second. "You can keep the knife."

I stand shaking, not knowing what to do, slowly closing the blade. "I'm sorry."

He peels off two dollar bills and offers them to me.

"Go where you want and get some grub."

"It's okay. I can manage."

He is insisting, pushing the money at me, warning me, like my father—to take the money and stay out of trouble. No no no, and I am jumping down to the icy street, sliding down, leaping up and rushing off in a swirl of snow, more ashamed and frightened than I have ever been in my life.

*Then said Pilate unto them, Take ye him, and judge him according to your law. The Jews therefore said unto him, It is not lawful for us to put any man to death.* Obviously they have fed him well; the guards strain to secure the straps around his sagging belly. Obligingly he inhales deeply as they snap the buckle and strap down his shoulders and legs. Two of the guards are leaving, but one lingers to adjust the stethoscope over the heart. There must be a precise moment of death to enter into the records. *The Lord is my shepherd; I shall not want. He maketh me to lie down in green pastures: he leadeth me beside still waters.* The guard is advising him, or warning him, to inhale "it" quickly, to get it over with fast. And, as he is leaving, he pats the man's back. But wait: the condemned man is asking for something and there is a flurry of movement outside the door. It must have been a Bible that he asked for; one is being thrust into the cubicle and the guard is placing it firmly in his hands. The guard is out now, closing the door. And at last he sits alone, head bowed, thumbing the Bible—thumbing and thumbing, awaiting death. They are sealing the door. What are his thoughts? Mine, agitated by this stranger who is about to die, race backward again, backward to a Chicago flophouse. Me, a boy again in the dirt and filth, broom in hand demanding my week's pay from Big John the boss, surly and drunk Big John charging me like a bull pummeling my face my body slamming me into the wall and kneeing me to the floor you black sonofabitch I'm not paying you a cent! Get the hell out of here before I kill you kill you kill you! And I run up the stairs and get his gun I rush down and point it at his heart and watch him shake from fear from rage I don't want to shoot but if he charges me I will pull the trigger he lunges up and I knock him sideways with the butt of the gun and he tries again and I swing viciously and catch him on the temple and he collapses in a heap on the floor. I'm running running running waiting for the siren but none comes. I pitch the gun sideways over the river bridge into the water, and then I run on.

And the man thumbs on as a tear rolls down his cheek —Samuel, Kings, Chronicles, Ezra, Esther, Job, Psalms. *He restoreth my soul; he leadeth me in the paths of righteousness for his name's sake.* In the glass I perceive my own image, and there distorted in the reflection the other witnesses, chalk-white in the nauseous green. Proverbs, Isaiah, Jeremiah (the warden's arm is rising), Lamentations. *Yea, though I walk through the valley of the shadow of death, I will fear no evil: for thou art with me; thy rod and thy staff they. . . .* The warden's arm drops. The pellet drops. The gas should be rising. Yes, his head just snapped backward. The thumb digs into Lamentations. And the Bible, falling free, snaps shut. There is intense quivering from the top of the head to the neck. His nervous system is being eaten away. *Thou preparest a table before me in the presence of mine enemies: thou anointest my head with oil; my cup runneth over.* The quivering reaches his belly, his hips, his knees, his legs; and there is one final spasm of protest as it reaches his toes. He is still. *And I will dwell in the house of the Lord for ever.*

It is over. Without reason he murdered a stranger; his judgment was served as dispassionately. How useless now, for him slumped there in death, that I fail to distinguish the profanity of one act from the profanity of the other. It seems, to my disordered thinking, that one evil, cloaked in cold judicial morality, has just fed upon another. As we file out, I sense that our young guard is pleased with the pain on my face. He wants to know if I enjoyed the show. I won't answer. "Too bad you wasn't around a few weeks ago when two other colored boys went at the same time. One cut his jugular with a razor blade before we could strap him down and blood was all over the windows, guards and chairs, and he was crying, 'Don't kill me, don't kill me,' and the other one was laughing like a hyena and hollering, 'Come on, man. Don't let whitey think you're scared'—and he kept laughing right up to the end."

Life, so precious, seems for the instant so absurdly

cheap. I keep walking, hearing, holding the silence we have been instructed to hold. The prison gates have closed behind us. The green chamber where we left him is silent. The killing gas, having done its job, is now being sucked to its own death. It seems ages ago since his small finger jerked upward after the other parts of him were dead. But his body is still warm with the life we took from him, still creased where the straps cut into the flesh. His soul can't be far away. Perhaps it hovers above, looking down upon the vacant body, indifferent to a God who would assign it to such anguish; damning the fallen Bible that holds the Commandment we have just violated.

# 2. The Black Muslims

MAY, 1963

*When blood flowed in the streets of Birmingham and black demonstrators filled prisons all over the South, the cry of the Black Muslims rose to its highest pitch. Obscure and overlooked since they had banded together in the early 1930s, they swept into prominence as blacks became increasingly impatient. Elijah Muhammad, the leader of the sect, was the messenger of a black Allah with a bitter doctrine: expect hate and violence from the whites—and be ready to return them. He preached separation from the white man's world and demanded an all-black nation inside the United States. Many blacks were in a mood to respond to this angry credo. The Muslims grew. Middle-class blacks, and black politicians who had shrugged off the movement for so long, suddenly began to court it.*

*The angry spokesman and troubleshooter for the sect was Malcolm X; I first saw him on a Harlem street corner one winter night. Shouting over the heads of half a thousand blacks, he pointed to a cordon of white policemen who stood to the rear. "You white devils know where the dope is! You know where the whores and pimps are! You know where the dope pushers and numbers racketeers are!*

*You're a rotten part of them! You are the rotten white devils who they pay to stay in business! We Muslims defy you! We blacks in the community are tired of you being on our backs! Touch a Muslim and may Allah have mercy on your soul!"*

I shot a glance at the cops. They stood silent, refusing to even look at their tormentor. But the hatred in their eyes matched the venom in Malcolm's voice and words. *That's one crazy black man,* I thought. *He'll be lucky to live out the winter.*

But I saw Malcolm X again the following spring, when I told him that I wanted very much to do a story on the Muslims. Malcolm told me only Elijah Muhammad could give me access to their closed world, a world which up to that time had been barred to all outsiders. Together we flew to Arizona to seek Elijah Muhammad's permission. As the plane banked for a landing I asked Malcolm what he thought my chances were. "Sir," he answered (it was always "Sir" in our early meetings), "it might be fatal to try and second-guess the Messenger. We will just have to wait and see."

*A*s I flew back from Phoenix, across this white Christian nation, I tried to summarize my impressions of Elijah Muhammad, whom I had just met for the first time—and to guess what he thought of me. He had made his mission and prophecy clear: as "spiritual head of the Muslims in the Western world," he would lead the black man out of his hell on earth. Both his manner and speech were subdued, but his condemnation of the "enemy" was ardent.

"The white devil's day is over," he said, "There is none a black man can trust. He was given six thousand years to rule. His time was up in nineteen fourteen. These are his years of grace—seventy of them. He's already used up most of those years trapping and murdering the black nations by the hundreds of thousands. Now he's worried, worried about the black man getting his revenge."

Although I was a Black Man in White Man's clothing, sent by the very "devils" he criticized so much, he made no attempts to convert me. Once he warned, "Don't forget, young man. You've been living in the white Christians' world for a long time. Don't let them blind you. You don't need them."

But he seemed to regard me with neither favor nor scorn. He said neither yes nor no to my request for permission to do a report on the internal workings of the Movement. Muhammad had consented to see me and expose me to his doctrine; then, in a matter-of-fact way, he had let me know exactly where he stood. Now, as I flew back to New York to await his decision, somehow I felt scorched from the heat of his inner burning.

The pilot announced our position over Chicago and I looked down, thinking of the three years I had lived in the infamous black belt of that city. I remembered the filth, fear, poverty, evictions and bloodshed; the rackets, police brutality, store-front churches—voices within praying, singing, shouting for mercy. I remembered the rat-infested tenements, the cold nights of winter when the hawk of misery spread his wings over the shivering black ghetto—and then the robberies and murders that followed, sometimes for food alone. Mostly I remembered the hopelessness that seeped into the black souls of that jungle. Now, from this height, Chicago shone clean in the afternoon sunlight. But I knew that, within the brightness below, torment and suffering filled the lives of thousands.

With my emotions oddly mixed of tenderness, pain and resentment, I wondered what Elijah Muhammad's words meant to those who had great reason to suffer. The soft-spoken, angry words kept coming back again and again. I wondered whether or not my achievements in the white world had cost me a certain objectivity. I could not deny that I had stepped a great distance from the mainstream of Negro life, not by intention but by circumstance. In fulfilling my artistic and professional ambitions in the white man's world, I had had to become completely involved in it.

At the beginning of my career I missed the soft, easy laughter of Harlem and the security of black friends about me. Although en route to my home in Westchester I occasionally drove through Harlem in those days, there was hardly ever enough time to become a physical part of it again. Eventually I found myself on a plateau of loneliness, not knowing really where I belonged. In one

world I was a social oddity. In the other I was almost a stranger.

Many times I wondered whether my achievement was worth the loneliness I experienced, but now I realize the price was small. This same experience has taught me that there is nothing ignoble about a black man climbing from the troubled darkness on a white man's ladder, providing he doesn't forsake the others who, subsequently, must escape that same darkness.

In time the word came from Phoenix: Elijah Muhammad had found me worthy of his confidence. I could start my report. Mine was a strange journey through this secret state of Muslim mosques, where drillmasters and judo experts trained an elite guard called the Fruit of Islam. A tight discipline permeated the sect. Profanity, smoking, liquor and drugs were forbidden, as were music, singing and dancing, since they emphasized the white man's image of the black man. The Muslim's creed offered no happiness in an afterlife. Its rewards were guaranteed only in its own world, a world sternly puritanical yet surrounded by the constant threat of violence. The police were its openly declared enemies. For the next few months I was to melt into the Muslim organization and examine its aims, its laws and the legends surrounding it. I was to eat in its restaurants, attend its rallies and most secret ceremonies. I came to know entire families who were devout members. And all the while I attempted

to assess its meaning to America and to the American Negro—and to myself.

What was Elijah Muhammad's real purpose? Was his movement indeed gaining countless unshakable adherents? And why was his voice, barely audible in person, screaming loudest in the wilderness, often drowning out the more conservative voices of the N.A.A.C.P., the Urban League and other highly respected Negro organizations?

I asked Malcolm X, who served as my guide through the intricacies of Islam, some of these same questions late one night as we drove along the noisy streets of Harlem. He replied, "The thinking American Negro realizes that only Elijah Muhammad offers him a solid, united front. He is tired of the unfulfilled promises of the lethargic, so-called Negro leaders who have been so thoroughly brainwashed by the American whites. 'Have patience,' they say, 'everything is going to be all right.'

"The black man in this country has been sitting on the hot stove for nearly four hundred years. And no matter how fast the brainwashers and the brainwashed think they are helping him advance, it's still too slow for the man whose behind is burning on that hot stove!"

Malcolm's caustic reply was to take on more meaning, more truth, as I read the daily newspaper accounts of the black man's interminable suffering in the South. The "white devil" seemed determined to live up to Malcolm's predictions. I thought of my younger son, who had just received a notice from the draft board, and I thought of the words of Malcolm X:

"The black man has died under the flag. His women have been raped under it. He has been oppressed, starved and beaten under it—and still after what happened in Mississippi they'll ask him to fight their enemies under it. I'll do my fighting right here at home, where the enemy looks me in the eye every day of my life. I'm not talking against the flag. I'm talking *about* it!"

Abruptly I checked the flow of corrosive thoughts. Was I becoming too receptive to the Muslim doctrine? I began prodding myself into a more argumentative mood, re-examining my feelings so that I might honestly assess the moral convictions I had developed so painfully through the years. When I was young—penniless and obsessed with the ambition to become a photographer—Harvey Goldstein, a white man, gave me my first decent camera, along with invaluable guidance in using it. Later, William G. Haygood, a white Southerner, encouraged me and helped me win the first Julius Rosenwald Fellowship in photography. Julio de Diego, the Spanish painter, offered inspiration and advice. Jack Delano, a Jew, guided me toward the Farm Security Administration, where I fell under the influence of Roy Stryker, a Dutchman from Colorado, who taught me more about democracy and its almost infinite potential than any person I've met since.

In the course of a career that has thrust me into contact with virtually every kind of person and has taken me several times around the world, I have come to realize the universality of man.

No, I could no more dismiss the events that molded

me than I could cast off the cloak of my skin—no matter how appealing Malcolm X was as an individual or as a minister of Muhammad.

Yet there must be, I concluded, some reason why the Muslims struck a responsive chord, not only in me but in so many Negroes moving in sophisticated circles who previously had held themselves aloof from the day-to-day aspects of "the problem." It came as a shock, one afternoon at a chic outdoor party, to hear well-to-do Negro women extolling black nationalism. One matron threatened to join the New York mosque of the Muslims. I heard another berate a blond woman for the Caucasians' treatment of "her people." "You mean, *our* people," retorted the fair-skinned lady. "I happen to be Negro too."

The hostess laughed and nudged me. "Neither she nor anyone in her family would have admitted that ten years ago!"

The Muslims, with their sharp and unrelenting attack, their aggressive racial pride, have awakened Negroes long insulated by their middle-class possessions and aspirations. Behind the Islamic chanting and the semimilitary ritual there lies a cause—one which calls to Negro slum dwellers and suburbanites alike.

Particularly strong is the attraction for the Negro "lowest down on the totem pole," as labor leader A. Philip Randolph has described them. By their very nature the N.A.A.C.P. and the Urban League cannot match the impact of the Black Muslims. Their leaders do not have the hour-by-hour contact with people who, like the Muslims,

suffer the problem each and every day of their lives. While Roy Wilkins of the N.A.A.C.P. is attending an integrated social gathering, or is conferring with constitutional lawyers on vital civil rights issues, Malcolm X of the Muslims is visiting prisoners in jail or a destitute family or addressing a crowd of Negroes on a street corner:

"Justice now! Freedom now! Not when the white man feels he is finally ready to give it to us!"

Although Malcolm X is the most articulate spokesman in the movement, there are some areas of Muslim philosophy into which he does not venture. One day en route to the Temple No. 7 Restaurant in Harlem I asked him, "Exactly what are Mr. Muhammad's ultimate aims?"

He paused for a moment. "It's best that you ask him on your next visit," he replied. "He loves to explain this himself. But I will tell you that he intends to unite every American black man, whether he be a Muslim, a Methodist or a Catholic. Mr. Muhammad teaches that we cannot afford the luxury of economic, religious or political difference. We must sit in counsel if we are to attain our freedom.

"Remember," Malcolm X cautioned as I left the restaurant. "To try to go it alone is to doom yourself to failure. The black attorneys, students, writers, clergy, teachers and all the rest must unite as one and take the Muslim leadership for their own salvation. If I have a bowl of soup, then you have a bowl of soup. If you die fighting for what is right, then I must die beside you—for I am your brother. You are a black man. The white man won't let you forget it. So know yourself and be yourself. We are of the black nation and we must recapture our rightful heritage and culture and live accordingly."

I started to hail a cab but Gladstone X, a Muslim who is close to Malcolm X, was already in the street, his arm raised and signaling. A taxi screeched to a stop and Gladstone opened the door for me. "Good night, brother," he called as the car pulled off.

I had just settled back when the driver, a big, broad-shouldered Negro, turned and spoke. "That was Malcolm X, wasn't it?"

"Yes, it was," I said. "Do you know him?"

"Oh, not personal like, but I hear him speakin' sometimes on the corner with the rest of those nationalist people."

"What do you think of him?"

"Me? Oh, I dig him the most. He's got somethin' goin' for you and me. He's the only one that makes any sense for my money."

"Are you a Muslim?"

"Who, me? Naw. I'm too busy makin' a buck to join anything. But those Muslims or Moslems, 'ever what you call 'em, make more sense to me than the N.A.A.C.P. and Urban League and all the rest of 'em put together. They're down on the good earth with the brother. They're for their own people and that Malcolm ain't afraid to tell Mr. Charlie, the FBI or the cops or nobody where to get off. You don't see him pussyfootin' round the whites like he's scared of 'em."

"Have they got many followers here in Harlem?"

"I don't know how many followers he's got, but he's sure got a hell of a lot of well-wishers."

"Do you go for all their teachings—like not smoking or drinking or eating pork or fornicating?"

"Well, I don't smoke or drink much, but I like my barbecue and I do like my women. That's about the only place the Muslims and I part company. As far as the white man is concerned, if I could get along without his dollar, I could get along without him."

"Some people say the Muslims hate all white people."

"Well, I don't know about that. But if they don't, they should, 'cause they sure don't waste no love on us. That's for sure!"

"But the Negro is making progress in this country," I reminded him. "And there are some good whites."

"Aw, yeah. And there's some good dogs, too, but all of 'em'll bite you if you don't watch 'em."

"What about the new Negro astronaut they have just selected for training?"

"Well, that's good . . . very good. But I wouldn't be surprised if they didn't put him and a Jew in one of those capsules together and blow it to hell and gone up to the moon—just to prove a white man's the only one can really make it!"

We were at my hotel now. I paid my fare and said, "How do you think we can solve the racial question?"

"Well, I'll tell you," the cabbie replied. "I used to live in Mobile and I lived in Memphis and I've lived in New

York for fifteen years. I've come to one conclusion. No matter where the white man is, he's the same—the only thing he respects is force. And the only thing's gonna change him is some lead in his belly."

He lifted a cigar box from the seat beside him and opened it. "I don't like to come downtown," he said. "See this?" A black revolver glistened in the street light. "I'm always afraid I'll use it. That's why I'm headin' back uptown 'fore I get in trouble."

As I left, two white men hailed the cab. The driver slammed the door, locked it and gunned the motor. "Goin' home!" he shouted back at them.

"The dirty black bastard!" one of the men mumbled as the cab roared off toward Central Park.

Recently I sat in a Los Angeles courtroom at the trial of fourteen Muslims charged with assault and interfering with an officer. They had been involved in an altercation with the police, during which one young Muslim, Ronald Stokes, was shot to death. (I had read the detailed account of the tragedy in the Muslims' newspaper, *Muhammad Speaks*. SEVEN UNARMED NEGROES SHOT IN COLD BLOOD BY LOS ANGELES POLICE! the red headline blared. The story charged that the police had entered the Muslims' temple during the fighting.) The courtroom was crowded to capacity with Negroes, not all of them Muslims.

I watched Malcolm X seated in the front row, directly

across from the all-white jury. His face was sphinxlike and his eyes never left Officer Donald Weese, the killer of Stokes, from the moment the policeman took the stand until he got off. During the preliminary hearings it had been established that Weese, though he knew the Muslims were unarmed, shot at least four other men besides Stokes and beat another one down with the butt of his gun. The following questions by Attorney Earl Broady and answers from Officer Weese are from the court records of the trial:

> *Question*—Mr. Weese, when you fired at Stokes, did you intend to hit him?
> *Answer*—Yes, I did.
> Q—Did you intend to hit him and kill him?
> A—Yes. The fact that I shot to stop and the fact that I shot to kill is one and the same, sir. I am not Hopalong Cassidy. I cannot distinguish between hitting an arm and so forth, sir. I aimed dead center and I hoped I hit.
> Q—You are saying, sir, to shoot to stop and to shoot to kill is one and the same thing in your mind?
> A—That is correct.
> Q—Did you feel to protect yourself and your partner it was necessary to kill these men?
> A—That is correct, sir.

Leaving the courthouse that evening, I recognized a white reporter who was covering the trial for one of the Los Angeles dailies.

"The Muslims are going to be convicted," he said. I asked him if he thought they were guilty as charged.\*

---

\* Twelve of them were convicted.

VICTIMS PAY $90,000 FOR "JUSTICE"
25c
EXTRA
25c
Muslim Story of:
SEVEN UNARMED NEGROES
IN COLD BLOOD BY
ANGELES POLICE

"The State has no case, none whatsoever, but they can't afford to lose this one. They've got to get those cops off or the Muslims can sue them for millions," he replied.

That evening I relayed the reporter's beliefs to Malcolm X, who said, "Oh, he told you the truth, brother. He was an honest devil, because that's what will happen—but things won't end there. Believe me."

A few days later I again accompanied Malcolm X to Phoenix, where Elijah Muhammad discussed the trial with more emotional intensity than I had seen him show before. "Every one of the Muslims," he said, "should have died before they allowed an aggressor to come into their mosque. That's the last retreat they have. They were fearless, but they didn't trust Allah completely. If they had, it would have been a different story. A true Muslim must trust completely in Allah."

Mr. Muhammad was weak from one of his periodic fasts, which had gone on for three days, and every so often spasmodic coughing forced him to leave the room. After each attack he returned to deride the "white devil." Although fatigue slowed his voice, he talked on, about the turmoil in Birmingham and other parts of the South. "There is one thing good about what is happening down there," he said. "The black man at last can see what the white man is really like, what he really feels about him. Birmingham bears witness to the fact that a white man is a devil and can't do right, what with water hoses stripping dresses from our women and our youth being chased and bitten by vicious dogs. At last the black man realizes he must fight for his rights if he is to attain them. The white man is more vicious than the dogs he sets upon us. He is never satisfied with a black man no matter what his position. You can lie down and let your back be his doormat, but soon he'll get tired of that and start kicking you. 'Turn over, nigger! You're layin' on the same side too long,' he'll say."

Before leaving Mr. Muhammad, I asked two questions I had been saving. First, "What is salvation for the black man?"

"We must accept Islam," he said crisply. "We are the initial people."

"Why?" I asked.

"Because it is something universal, wherein man submits himself completely to God—a black God."

Second, "What is your over-all purpose—your goal?"

"Universal peace and brotherly love—two things the white man will never be able to accept."

It was nearing plane time. A white-suited chauffeur ushered us out toward Muhammad's limousine. I got in, and through the rear window I could see him and Malcolm X warmly embracing, their cheeks touching as they bade farewell.

Not all of Elijah Muhammad's aims and motives are clear to me. Much of his religious philosophy appears naïve and thoroughly confusing. It is obvious from which stratum of Negro society he hopes to draw support for his program: the indigent, unprivileged blacks, those still seeking a messiah to lead them into a promised land of "freedom, justice and equality."

The Muslims insist that only within a separate state can their ultimate goal be achieved. They deride the "passive resistance" preached by Martin Luther King, Jr. Malcolm X once said of King's attitude, "There is no philosophy more befitting the white man's tactics for keeping his foot on the black man's neck. If you tell someone he resembles Hannibal or Gandhi long enough, he starts believing it—even begins to act like it. But there is a big difference in the passiveness of King and the passiveness of Gandhi. Gandhi was a big dark elephant sitting on a little white mouse. King is a little black mouse sitting on top of a big white elephant."

But with the passiveness of King and the extremism of Muhammad, the Negro rebellion has come alive. Fire hoses, police dogs, mobs or guns can't put it down. The Muslims, the N.A.A.C.P., the Urban League, Black Nationalist groups, the sit-inners, sit-downers, Freedom Riders and what-have-you are all compelled into a vortex of common protest. Black people who only a few months ago spoke with polite moderation are suddenly clamoring for freedom.

The leaders have lost control; instead of leading the black people they are being pulled along after them, like leaves caught up in the wake of a speeding car. Even Martin Luther King is seeing his nonviolence movement hopelessly swept into a long-fomenting universal revolt. As the Negro pushes on, the resistance of the Deep

South will surely stiffen. Violence and chaos are inevitable. Anyone who can't sense it is either naïve or afraid to face the uncomfortable fact. Racial strife is possible all over this land. Have we so very quickly forgotten the Harlem, Chicago, Tulsa and Detroit riots in the earlier days of our troubled generation?

"Even here in the North the 'enemy' is plentiful!" screams Malcolm X.

He is right. Because for all the civil rights laws and the absence of Jim Crow signs in the North, the black man is still living the last-hired, first-fired, ghetto existence of a second-class citizen. His children are idling into delinquency and crime; in too many places they attend schools as inferior and as neatly segregated as any in the deepest South. The revolt in Englewood, New Jersey, against segregated schools there is just as important to the cause as the revolt in Birmingham or Nashville. Truly, there has been no time like this in the United States since the Civil War.

Most of us are wondering about the "new" Negro—and how he got this way. But he isn't new, and he didn't get this way overnight. He has been stirring for a long time, while his country tucked the Emancipation Proclamation under her head for a pillow and went to sleep. The historic Supreme Court decision of 1954 disturbed her repose, but that was all. Now she has been jolted awake by a black militancy that will surely test her democratic conscience.

I remember once standing in a Paris bar with Todd

Webb, a white man, trying to convince a Russian student that Todd and I were truly friends, that we had been so even in America. The Russian only laughed at both of us. "Ha! I read about America, you know. You are together here, but in America you stand far apart. Don't think you fool me."

And how pathetically torn I was trying to defend America against the criticisms of Europeans when papers all over the world carried the story of the lynching of the Negro boy, Emmett Till!

I also recall the time in Washington, D.C., when John Vachon, another white friend, and I walked into a Negro restaurant late one cold night. We were famished, but the owner became abusive and ordered us both out. I tried to get him to sell my friend some ribs. "Not even to take out," he said bitterly. "I'll go *his* people one better."

The times cry out for bold, principled leadership of a kind that has never really been attempted in this country before. After Attorney General Robert Kennedy ran head-on into the fanatical opposition of Alabama's Governor George Wallace on the desegregation issue, the President's brother was quoted as saying, "It's like a foreign country. There's no communication. What do you do?"

You keep trying, Mr. Kennedy. You keep going back for more, again and again, until you begin to realize what it is like for a black man to "go slow," to "take it easy" while under the boot heel of a racist like "Bull" Connor. Go down there sometime when the fire hoses are on full blast, when the dogs are snarling and tearing black flesh, when women, men and children are on their knees singing, crying and praying for deliverance from the agony of this brutal land. Then go back and tell the President that if it is greatness he seeks, this indeed is his chance for it.

I have had faith in America for as long as I can remember. But I have also been angry—even bitter. It is now time for America to justify this belief I have in her, to show me I have not believed in vain. I want my children and their children to keep this faith flowing through their veins. But in all honesty I cannot ask of them love for a country incapable of returning their love.

As for the Muslims, I dislike the fact that they exist, but I also feel this way about the N.A.A.C.P., CORE, the Urban League, B'nai B'rith, the Sons and Daughters of Erin or any such group. I deplore the conditions that necessitate their existence. If and when all such organizations feel they can safely fold their tents, I believe the Muslims will begin folding theirs.

Nobody can speed this day any quicker than the white American. He should remember that the main reason for the racial strife throughout the South and parts of the North is the Negro's black skin. The Negro can't change his color; the white man must change his attitude toward that black skin. And the Negro can't go around believing that every white man who does not invite him home to dinner is his enemy.

And I, for one, don't intend to join the Muslims. I sympathize with much of what they say, but I also disagree with much of what they say.

I wouldn't follow Elijah Muhammad or Malcolm X into a Black State—even if they achieve such a complete separation. I've worked too hard for a place in this present society. Furthermore, such a hostile frontier would only bristle even more with hatred and potential violence. Nor will I condemn all whites for the violent acts of their brothers against the Negro people. Not just yet, anyway.

Nevertheless, to the Muslims I acknowledge that the circumstance of common struggle has willed us brothers. I know that if unholy violence should erupt—and I pray it won't—this same circumstance will place me, reluctantly, beside them. Although I won't allow them to be my keeper, I am, inherently, their brother.

Late one evening not long ago Malcolm X and I were driving into New York City from Brooklyn. We were talked out, and I drowsed as he fought the headlight glare of oncoming traffic. Unexpectedly he said, "We sent a little white college girl out of the restaurant in tears today." I listened uneasily, bracing myself for another diatribe against a presumptuous, if well-meaning "devil."

But Malcolm, speaking with a gentleness he rarely exhibits when discussing whites, hastened to assure me that it was nothing any Muslim had said against her. "She had come in to see if there wasn't something she and her college friends could do to help Muslims and the whites get together," he explained.

"That's nice," I said, pushing up in my seat. "What did you say?"

I am positive he was unaware of the trace of melancholy in his voice as he answered, "I told her that there was no chance—not the ghost of a chance. She started crying, then she turned and went out."

# 3. The Death of Malcolm X

*MARCH, 1965*

*A shocked country mourning the death of President Kennedy was further shocked by Malcolm X's widely quoted statement that the assassination was "chickens coming home to roost." This statement was assumed to be the reason for Malcolm X's expulsion from the Black Muslims early in 1965.*

*According to Malcolm, the meaning of his words was blown far out of proportion. "I was saying that American whites, no longer content to kill blacks, were now murdering each other—even their President." He told me soon after breaking with the Muslims to form his own militant cadre, "It was a lie, a shallow pretense to get me out of the movement. It's simple; Elijah Muhammad was out to get me."*

*No one outside of the Muslims really knew why he was ousted. Malcolm wasn't too clear about it himself. For a long time he said he actually believed that his reinstatement as the Number One minister was imminent. The permanence of the break, he said, "finally dawned on me when they tried to burn my house down."*

*Shortly thereafter Malcolm X lay dying on the stage of*

*a Manhattan auditorium, his life oozing out through gun-
shot wounds in his chest. The most powerful voice in the
black revolt had been stilled by pistol and shotgun blasts
—triggered by members of his own race. But most blacks
today feel that influential whites helped prepare the violent execution. The CIA and certain law-enforcement
agencies within the government do not escape their sus-
picion. For a short time after Malcolm X's death the black
community verged on a fratricidal war, but except for a
few minor skirmishes, nothing happened. The slain leader
was given a funeral befitting a fallen hero. Monuments to
his memory are mushrooming all over the country. It
seems that he has become more powerful in death than
he was in life, a black martyr to the black man's cry for
justice.*

**D**eath was surely absent from his face two
days before they killed him. He appeared calm and some-
what resplendent with his goatee and astrakhan hat.
Much of the old hostility and bitterness seemed to have
left him, but the fire and confidence were still there.
We talked of those months two years ago when I had
traveled with him through the closed world of Muslimism,
trying to understand it. I remembered Malcolm, sweat
beading on his hard-muscled face, his fist slashing the
air in front of his audience: "Hell is when you don't have

justice! And when you don't have equality, that's hell! And the devil is the one who robs you of your right to be a human being! I don't have to tell you who the devil is. You know who the devil is!" (*"Yes, Brother Malcolm! Tell 'em like it is!"*)

Malcolm said to me now, "That was a bad scene, brother. The sickness and madness of those days—I'm glad to be free of them. It's a time for martyrs now. And if I'm to be one, it will be in the cause of brotherhood. That's the only thing that can save this country. I've learned it the hard way—but I've learned it. And that's the significant thing."

I was struck by the change, and I felt he was sincere, but couldn't his disenchantment with Elijah Muhammad have forced him into another type of opportunism? As recently as December 20 he had yelled at a Harlem rally: "We need a Mau Mau to win freedom and equality in the United States! . . ." There was an inconsistency here. Could he, in his dread of being pushed into obscurity, have trumped up another type of zealotry? I doubted it. He was caught, it seemed, in a new idealism. And, as time bore out, he had given me the essence of what was to have been his brotherhood speech—the one his killers silenced. It was this intentness on brotherhood that cost him his life. For Malcolm, over the objections of his bodyguards, was to rule against anyone being searched before entering the hall that fateful day: "We don't want people feeling uneasy," he said. "We must create an image that makes people feel at home."

"Is it really true that the Black Muslims are out to get you?" I asked.

"It's as true as we are standing here. They've tried it twice in the last two weeks."

"What about police protection?"

He laughed. "Brother, nobody can protect you from a Muslim but a Muslim—or someone trained in Muslim tactics. I know. I invented many of those tactics."

"Don't you have any protection at all?"

He laughed again. "Oh, there are hunters and there are those who hunt the hunters. But the odds are certainly with those who are most skilled at the game."

He explained that he was now ready to provide a single, unifying platform for all our people, free of political, religious and economic differences. "One big force under one banner," he called it. He was convinced that whatever mistakes he had made after leaving Elijah Muhammad had been in the name of brotherhood. "Now it looks like this brotherhood I wanted so badly has got me in a jam," he said.

Within the last year he had sent me postcards from Saudi Arabia, Kuwait, Ethiopia, Kenya, Nigeria, Ghana and Tanganyika, and I thanked him for them.

"Everybody's wondering why I've been going back and forth to Africa. Well, first I went to Mecca to get closer to the orthodox religion of Islam. I wanted first-hand views of the African leaders—their problems are inseparable from ours. The cords of bigotry and prejudice here can be cut with the same blade. We have to keep

that blade sharp and share it with one another." Now he
was sounding like the old Malcolm: "Strangely enough,
listening to leaders like Nasser, Ben Bella and Nkrumah
awakened me to the dangers of racism. I realized racism
isn't just a black and white problem. It's brought blood
baths to about every nation on earth at one time or
another."

He stopped and remained silent for a few moments.
"Brother," he said finally, "remember the white college
girl who wanted to help the Muslims and the whites get
together—and I told her there wasn't a ghost of a chance
and she went away crying?"

"Yes."

"Well, I've lived to regret that incident. In many parts
of the African continent I saw white students helping
black people. Something like this kills a lot of argument.
I did many things as a Muslim that I'm sorry for now. I
was a zombie then—like all Muslims—I was hypnotized,
pointed in a certain direction and told to march. Well, I
guess a man's entitled to make a fool of himself if he's
ready to pay the cost. It cost me twelve years."

As we parted he laid his hand on my shoulder, looked
into my eyes and said, "A salaam alaikem, brother."

"And may peace be with you, Malcolm," I answered.

Driving home from that last meeting with Malcolm,
I realized once more that, despite his extremism and in-
consistencies, I liked and admired him. A certain humility
was wed to his arrogance. I assumed that his bitterness
must have come from his tragic early life. His home in

East Lansing, Michigan, was burned to the ground by white racists. He had lived for many years with the belief that whites had bludgeoned his father to death and left his body on the tracks to be run over by a streetcar.

Malcolm's years of ranting against the "white devils" helped create the climate of violence that finally killed him, but the private man was not a violent one. He was brilliant, ambitious and honest. And he was fearless. He said what most of us black folk were afraid to say publicly. When he told off "a head-whipping cop"—as he described him—his tongue was coupled with a million other black tongues. When he condemned the bosses of the "rat-infested ghetto," a Harlemful of fervid "Amens" could be heard ricocheting off the squalid tenements.

I remember Malcolm's complete devotion to Elijah Muhammad and his words when he was serving as the Muslims' spokesman: "All that Muhammad is trying to do is clean up the mess the white man has made, and the white man should give him credit. He shouldn't run around here calling [Muhammad] a racist and a hate-teacher. White man, call yourself a hate-teacher because you invented hate. Call yourself a racist because you invented the race problem."

Malcolm was not after power in the Muslim organization, but his unquestioning belief in the movement, his personal charm, his remarkable ability to captivate an audience brought him that power. With Elijah aging and ailing, Malcolm became the obvious choice as his successor. But his power and prominence also made him a marked man in the tightly disciplined society. His downfall had started even before his notorious comment on President Kennedy's assassination ("Chickens coming home to roost never did make me sad; they've always made me glad!"). But with that statement he unwittingly made himself more vulnerable.

On the night of Malcolm's death, at the home of friends where his family had taken refuge, I sat with his wife, Betty, his two oldest children and a group of his stunned followers, watching a television review of his stormy life. When his image appeared on the screen, blasting away at the injustices of "the enemy," a powerfully built man sitting near me said softly, "Tell 'em like it is, Brother Malcolm, tell 'em like it is."

The program ended and Betty got up and walked slowly to the kitchen and stood staring at the wall. Six-year-old Attallah followed and took her mother's hand. "Is Daddy coming back after his speech, Momma?"

Betty put her arms around the child and dropped her head on the refrigerator. "He tried to prepare me for this day," she said. "But I couldn't bring myself to listen. I'd just walk out of the room. The other day—after they tried to bomb us out of the house—was the only time I could stay and listen. I just closed my eyes and hung onto everything he said. I was prepared. That's why I'm ashamed I cried over him when he was lying there all shot up."

Only Qubilah, the four-year-old, seemed to understand

that her father wouldn't come again. She tugged at her mother's skirt. "Please don't go out, Momma."

"I won't go, baby. Momma won't go out." She gently pushed the child's head into her lap and told her to go to sleep.

"He was always away," Betty went on, "but I knew he would always come back. We loved each other. He was honest—too honest for his own good, I think sometimes." I started to leave and she said, "I only hope the child I'm carrying is just like his father."

"I hope you get your wish," I said.

I rode back to the city with the heavy-set man who had sat near me during the telecast. He slumped in disgust and guilt. "We could have saved him. We could have saved him," he kept mumbling. "How stupid. How stupid."

"What happens now?" I asked.

"Plenty, brother, plenty. *They* made a mistake. We'll rally now like one big bomb. Those zombies are the biggest obstacle in the progress of our people. They're like quicksand. They swallow up people by the dozens. I got into the organization thinking I was going to help promote progress and all the stuff they hand you. The next thing I knew, I was hawking their lying newspaper."

"So, what happens now?" I repeated.

"Six brothers are already on their way for the main visit."

"Main visit?"

"There's always been a standing order. If anything happens to Brother Malcolm, six brothers catch the first plane to Chicago, or Phoenix—wherever he's at."

"Elijah Muhammad, you mean?"

"He's the top zombie. He's the first to be visited."

I thought back to the time in Phoenix when I last saw Muhammad and Malcolm together—the two men warmly embracing, their cheeks touching in farewell. I felt empty.

"And after him?" I asked.

"The names on Brother Malcolm's list—the ones who were trying to kill him."

The list, as the newspapers reported, was taken from Malcolm's pocket as he lay dying.

"They know who they are. They've been properly notified," he said solemnly. The list also includes the principal targets for vengeance: the *Muhammad Speaks* newspaper office, the Shabazz Restaurant, Mosque No. 7. "If they're able to hold their meetings at the mosque after tomorrow night," the man said, "I'll join up with them again. Brother, that place will be no more."

I took his word for it—and my despair deepened.

# 4. Redemption of a Champion

SEPTEMBER, 1966

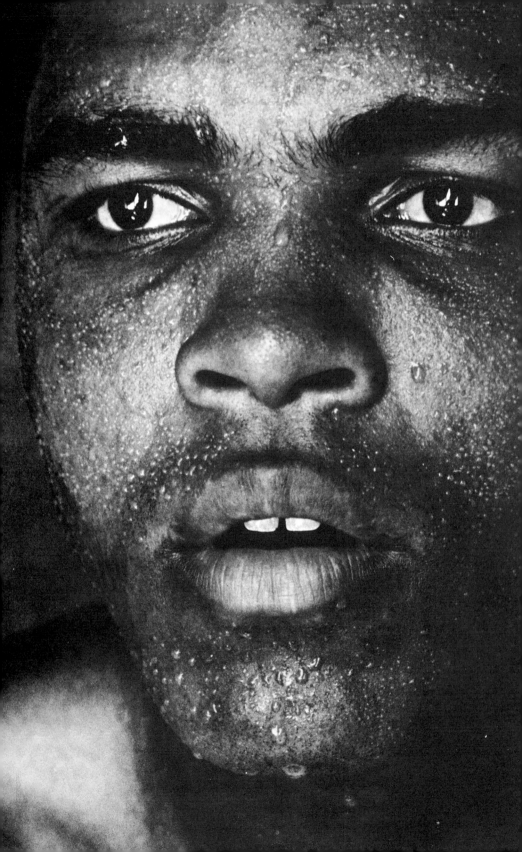

*L*ONDON—late spring. A knock came on the door as I was packing my bags and Muhammad Ali came dancing into the hotel room—"*Whoomp whoomp whoomp*"—throwing lefts and rights close to my head. His young face was free of the fury it held a few hours before when he was beating Henry Cooper. Most of London was still sleeping off the defeat of its champion. And considering the physical demands of the fight, and the yelling, shoving mobs that had clawed at him later, I thought Muhammad would be sleeping too. But here he was, the improbable Louisville Kid, come to say a quick good-by.

"Go—o-ord-on P-a-a-rks." He strung out my name for several seconds, flopped across both twin beds and took a piece of paper from his pocket. "Here's the poem I've been promising you. Want to hear it?" Before I could answer he was reading.

> "Since I won't let critics seal my fate
> They keep hollering I'm full of hate.
> But they don't really hurt me none
> 'Cause I'm doing good and having fun.

And fun to me is something bigger
Than what those critics fail to figure.
Fun to me is lots of things
And along with it some good I bring.
Yet while I'm busy helping my people
These critics keep writing I'm deceitful.
But I can take it on the chin
And that's the honest truth, my friend.
Now from Muhammad you just heard
The latest and the truest word.
So when they ask you what's the latest
Just say 'Ask Ali. He's still the greatest.'"

"Well, how'd you like it?" he asked proudly.

"Just fine." I edged toward the subject that was really on my mind. "And you were good with the press after the fight."

"Yeh? Guess I said all the right things. Well, the loud talk and everything is over now. Just being myself from now on—a good-acting champ."

Right. Just right. Exactly what I wanted to hear him say. The question was how deep it all went. The situation reminded me of the final moments I had spent with my son David, before he went off to the Army. (Muhammad and David resemble one another, not only physically but in the way they walk and gesture.) Only this time I didn't offer any advice. I wanted to. I wanted to say: "Just remember—*don't let reporters rile you. Don't always ham it up for the cameras. Listen to your trainers. Be careful about your draft situation.*" But I had learned that this boy, unlike my son, was not receptive to outright advice; even when you gave it gently you got silence—no response at all.

Now he jumped up suddenly, handed me the poem and gave me a bear hug. "Well, so long, champ," he said. Then, throwing punches again, he danced out the door.

I had met Muhammad Ali in Miami a month earlier, when he started training for Cooper, the first of his summer series of overseas fights. His public image was then in tatters. He stood accused in the press of sins ranging from talking too much to outright antiwhite bigotry. There had been rumblings of dislike for him ever since he became a Muslim after the first Clay-Liston fight in February, 1964. Then, late last winter, when he declared, "I don't have no quarrel with those Vietcongs!" he became, in the public eye, not just a loud-mouthed kid but a "shameless traitor," as one paper put it.

At that point I began to feel a certain sympathy for him. I was not proud of him, as I had been proud of Joe Louis. Muhammad was a gifted black champion and I *wanted* him to be a hero, but he wasn't making it. I felt, however, that he could not possibly be quite so bad as he was made out to be in the press.

He lay on his bed, in the small bungalow he always rents in Miami, half-covered by a sheet, only his chest and his powerful bare shoulders exposed. He smiled broadly as I came in.

"Sit down," he said in a surprisingly soft voice. "They tell me you're the greatest."

There were no chairs, so I sat down on the bed beside him. He had a magazine in his hand and he pointed to a word in an article about him: "What's that mean?"

I studied the word for a second. "He's saying you're 'paradoxical,' that you aren't what you appear to be—sometimes."

"Uh huh. And just what does he mean by calling me a bigot?"

I thought of the word "racist," but I said, "He's accusing you of being just as intolerant against whites as they are to us." He went on like this for a while, asking questions but never commenting on the answers I gave.

At first I was puzzled. The conversation, if it could be called that, didn't seem to be getting anywhere. But after a time I realized that we were, in fact, *talking*—person to person, without any put-on at all—and that this was his way of saying that he trusted me. I felt free to tell him quite directly that I had come to Miami to see whether he was really as obnoxious as people were making him out to be.

"No need to beat around the bush, brother," he said quickly. "I know why you came." His head slid off the pillow close to the wall. "People," he went on more softly, "have wrote a lot of bad things about me. But nothin' they write is goin' to turn *everybody* against me. Every fight, the gates just get bigger and the White Hopes get fewer."

Then, in a great swoosh, he sprang out of bed. "Come on, man, let's go see a movie!"

In my rented Cadillac he flicked on the radio, and out blasted the voice of the late Sam Cooke with "Shake." (*"Listen while I talk to you; I'll tell you what we're gonna do. There's a new thing that's go-in' a-round—and I'll tell you what they're put-tin' down."*)

Muhammad began singing along with him. An announcer's voice cut in: "Cassius Clay returned to Miami today to start training for his forthcoming fight with Henry Cooper in London. Cassius. . . ."

The announcer went on, but the champion had stopped listening: "Cassius Clay! I'm on everybody's lips. But still they won't call me by my right name."

Now he was directing the driver: *"Turn right, brother.* A white man is something. Yes, really something. *Left here, brother.* There's pressures and strains when you're successful and controversial like me. Gotta always be so careful about how you act, what you say. Everybody's waitin' to burn you."

"Then why get burned so often?"

"Maybe, sometimes, I just like to see how people take it."

I wondered whether it was also to see if people really cared about him.

Muhammad's brow knitted when we hit the cinema district: "What's all those signs say?"

"There's *Cast a Giant Shadow.* Looks good," I said. "Or Paul Newman in *Harper.*"

"Naw, naw. Something rough—with ghosts, no love and sex and stuff. What's that? *Goliath and the Vampires.* That's for me brother! Find out when it starts."

"It's half over," I protested feebly.

"Come on. Let's go anyhow. The last half's always the best."

Later Muhammad chose to stroll through Miami's Negro section. The rented limousine crept along the street behind us while greetings came from all the doorways and windows.

*"Hi, champ."*

"Hi, baby. What's shakin'?"

*"Hi, Muhammad. Who's the greatest?"*

"Are you blind, man?"

*"Hey, champ, how many rounds for Cooper?"*

"If he tries to get rough—one's enough."

*"You're the greatest, baby!"*

He could no more escape that last line than he could his color.

"These people like me around when they've got trouble. Patterson, Joe Louis, Sammy Davis and other Negro bigwigs don't do that. Too busy cocktailin' with the whites. I don't need bodyguards. You don't need protection from people who *love* you."

I asked myself how he could believe that the sycophantic chatter we'd just heard was "love." Did he think that a good world was one filled with smiles and flattery —one where all things were bigger than life? I began to suspect so.

He trained hard. In the ring Muhammad let the sparring partners bull and spin him about as Cooper might do. He floated and ducked, causing them to miss badly. "Dance, baby, dance," his trainer, Angelo Dundee, purred from the corner.

"Hey, Angelo, could I have whipped Jack Johnson in his time?"

"Baby, you could have taken anybody in everybody's time."

"And that's the beautiful truth, brother," Rahaman, his sparring partner, cut in. Such questions, such answers, I realized, meant more to him than I had imagined in the beginning. Muhammad seemed to encourage it all. Often he had asked me, "Why would a big magazine like yours want to do a story on me? Am I really that big? Do people really want to know about me?" He expected affirmative answers and he nearly always got them. He clearly needed these assurances against the bad publicity he was getting.

Some days he would drive up to a schoolyard at recess. "Come here, all you beautiful black children!" And they came running as if he were about to hand out thousand-dollar bills. "Only difference in me and the Pied Piper is he didn't have no Cadillac," he would say. The adoring kids were more important to him than he was to them.

During those lazy afternoons he talked about that "crazy house" he wanted to build on a high hill—"where travelers could come by and say, 'That's where he lives, the heavyweight champion of the world.'" But just about

any topic outside of Muslimism, boxing or himself made him tune out.

One day several boys came into the yard and two of them started sparring. "Hey, stop that!" he shouted at them. "You don't fight your brother—even in play. Now come on inside and I'll let you see some movies—of me beatin' up the 'Bear' and the 'Rabbit.'"

He continued the lecture as he threaded the projector: "They've been lynching your pappys and grandpappys and rapin' your mothers and sisters down here for years. There's plenty people to fight besides your brother. Catch you at it again, I'm gonna bop your heads together. Now, I'm gonna show the second Liston fight first, 'cause it last just long enough to warm up the machine."

He started the film and began announcing over the commentator's voice: "Here we go! Look, children! Looks like a turtle chasin' a jackrabbit! Now, watch close or you won't see it! *Rat-a-tat! Bop!* There it is! Now watch that clown fall flat on his face. There he goes! *Wham!*"

Muhammad ran up to the movie screen: "Git up, you bum. Get up and fight!"

When Patterson appeared on the screen Muhammad scoffed, "There's the Rabbit. Listen at 'em cheer. They love him. He's their black White Hope, children! Poor sucker! Now, here I come! Boooo! Boooo! Boooo! Boooo! Listen at 'em give it to me!"

I watched him closely. There was no joy in his heckling. Nobody could like being booed that much, especially not someone so concerned about "love."

I myself had wanted Floyd to beat him that night, and I told Ali so. He smiled! "I beat him so bad his breath smelled like saddle soap."

However, that fight bugged him. He was still trying to explain it in his bedroom late that night: "Patterson had no business in that ring with me—after saying he was going to bring the title 'back to America.' But the crowd came for a show and I gave 'em one. 'Come on, sucker, git past that left,' I kept saying to him. The ref felt sorry for him and kept telling me to shut up. I felt sorry for him, too. Maybe that's why I couldn't freeze him. But they didn't call that Patterson-Johansson fight sadistic. The Rabbit went down seven times."

His eyelids dropped for a few seconds. He had talked himself out. There was a little snore and he nodded himself awake. Then, looking out the window, he said, "I liked Floyd. He oughta quit. He's made lots of money. They'll never treat him as bad as they treat me." Then he dug his head into the pillow and went to sleep.

Some mornings, while he was winding up his training in Miami, I came upon him with his hands lifted, facing the East, mumbling prayers to Allah. Sometimes he seemed morose and disgruntled with everything around him. Then he would be in high spirits again—laughing, chattering, dancing, shadow-boxing in his yard, in the street, wherever there was room to throw a punch. It was never easy to know which of his different selves would be visible at a given moment.

I never witnessed the hate he is assumed to have for whites. But I did see him stand in the burning sun for an hour, signing autographs for Southern white children. And I did go with him on a visit to a young white hemophiliac one afternoon. On leaving the boy and his parents he remarked, "There are some good white folks around." I said it was nice of him to have made the visit. "Well," he answered, "he must have been a nice kid to want to see me."

Now and then his thoughts seemed far away. He would drop a conversation in midsentence without reason. Even when there was a great deal of noise around him, he would remain mute, meditative. One evening, in such a mood, he invited me for a walk. Just minutes before, he had been rearranging his scrapbook and I asked him why he didn't have a secretary.

"Oh, people don't ask me for much outside of autographs," he said. "No speeches and such things." He thought about that for a few paces.

"Do you know that Martin Luther King was the only Negro leader who sent me a telegram when I became champion of the world? The only one. I was just a dumb kid then, thinking all of them would be so proud of me— me being the champ and everything. I expected too much."

"You're so young yet. There's plenty of time to change —if you really want to."

"I want to. I'm sure I want to," he said, as though trying to convince himself. I repeated that he had plenty of time left and that the world had a lot to offer him.

After an intent pause, he said, "Nobody in this world ever offered me anything except Elijah Muhammad. Nobody."

Later that night, I went with him to the local mosque meeting. Muhammad Ali was dressed in the blue serge uniform of the Fruit of Islam. And, like everyone else who attended, he raised his arms and allowed himself to be frisked according to strict custom. Here, for the first time, I saw Muhammad listening eagerly to what someone else had to say.

Lucius Bey, the Muslim minister in Miami, started slowly, in a deliberately restrained voice. But soon the intensity increased: "The black man is indeed the greatest! His genes are stronger! No white man can produce a baby darker than himself! The most beautiful women in the world are black!"

"*Teach, brother, teach!*" Muhammad's voice led all the rest in the chorus.

"They say we hate the white man. We don't hate the white man! We just hate the way he treats us!"

"*Tell 'em like it is, brother! Preach!*" Now it was a duet between Lucius Bey and Muhammad.

"Why is the white man so anxious about Elijah Muhammad changing our slave names? Why? Africans are from Africa! Japanese are from Japan! Swedes are from Sweden! Where are Negroes from! Negroia?"

"*Wake us up, brother! Wake us up!*"

"Right NOW, the white man's being run out of all the

black countries! And—now, listen to this—he wants us black people to go fight for him to stay there!"

Lucius Bey had hit home: *"Preach the truth! They want me to go right now!"*

"When the white man asks, 'What's your name?' and you say, 'Muhammad Ali,' they say, "That nigger's done woke up!' "

*"Preach! Preach! Preach!"*

Lucius Bey preached on—for an hour and a half.

Lucius Bey's "message" was still burning inside Muhammad the next day. Angelo got told off; sparring partners got their lumps; there was no horsing around in camp that day, no movies, no children. And he kept spewing the kind of comment that had already made him a villain in the press. By evening the bungalow was dead quiet.

My original notion that there might be a different kind of story in Muhammad Ali had almost evaporated. I was going back to New York the next morning, and there now hardly seemed any need for me to go on to London.

Then, just before I left to go to my hotel, I took a chance and said to him, "It's not only white people, but a lot of Negroes don't like the way you act."

That cut him, deep. He erupted: "What do they want? I ain't promoting alcohol and sex-hugging on some white woman's head! So what if I am the first black athlete to stand up and say what I feel! Maybe I'm like the Japanese flier who sacrifices himself so others can live!

"Hate! Hate! Hate! Who's got time to go around hatin'

whites all day! I don't hate lions either—but I know they'll bite! What does the white man care if I hate him, anyhow? He's got everything going for him—white Swan soap, Tarzan, Jesus, White Owl cigars, the white tornado, Snow White and her Seven Dwarfs! Angel food cake is white—devil's food cake is black, naturally!"

He ranted on and on. Lucius Bey's sermon had been tepid in comparison.

"One question before I go," I said after listening to him for most of an hour. "What about your draft situation?"

"What about it? How can I kill somebody when I pray five times a day for peace? Answer me! For two years the Army told everybody I was a nut. I was ashamed! My mother and father was ashamed! Now, suddenly, they decide I'm very wise—without even testing me again! I ain't scared. Just show me a soldier who'd like to be in that ring in my place!

"I see signs saying 'L.B.J., how many kids did you kill today?' Well, I ain't said nothing half that bad! I don't know nothing about Vietnam. Where is it anyway? Near China? Elijah Muhammad teaches us to fight only when we are attacked. My life is in his hands. That's the way it is. That's the way it's got to be."

He was wrapped up in himself—yes: still belligerent, still the mistreated kid against a hostile world. Yet, I reflected, he made some sense. The issue had never come up in my own home, but I knew I would have been ready to back up my own son if *he* had decided to resist going to Vietnam. Muhammad, however, was the heavyweight champion of the world. Did that give him a special responsibility to think and act differently? A lot of people clearly thought that it did. Yet I wasn't sure.

I didn't expect to see Muhammad again. But early the next morning there he was at my hotel door. "Hurry up, champ. You're about to miss your plane," he said. He spent the trip to the airport urging my driver through short cuts and around other cars. Carrying my bags, he ran all the way to the departure gate. Then his big hand held me back for an instant.

"I don't want to do anything that's going to hurt my people," he said. "I've been doing a lot of thinking since last night. I hope you'll be there in London."

I was sure he was making me a promise of some sort. "I'll be there," I said, and ran for the plane.


The London fog made Muhammad's plane four hours late. But the big crowd was still waiting. He stepped off smiling broadly, waving to all the cameras, reporters and the cheering crowd.

*"Got any predictions, champ?"*

"Nope."

*"Any poetry, champ?"*

"Nope. I'd have to keep my fingers together so you wouldn't say I was predicting."

*"You've toned down considerably—a different fellow."*

"It's just me, being myself."

Two days later the *Daily Telegraph* said: "Cassius Clay presented himself to an admiring British public yesterday as Muhammad Ali, a heavyweight champion of courtesy and charm."

He smiled when I showed him the newspaper: "Wait 'til the folks back home get a load of this."

"Do you really care about what they think back there?"

"I got a lot of boos," he said, "but—it's still home. I have to think about home."

The British found him to be a "decent chap." "Foxes" in miniskirts, mods and rockers chased him. His telephones rang all day and all night. The adoration finally took its toll.

"You got a extra bed at your hotel?" he asked me in desperation. I said I had.

"Then you've just took on a nonpaying guest, brother."

And each day after training he would come to my room, consume quarts of orange juice, check the sports pages and sleep. We talked of things we hadn't really talked about before—my family and his family. He woke up one afternoon and simply began talking about his childhood:

"I used to lay awake scared, thinking about somebody getting cut up or being lynched. Look like they was always black people I liked. And I always wanted to do something to help these people. But I was too little. Maybe now I can help by living up to what I'm supposed to be. I'm proud of my title and I guess I want people to be proud of me."

I was astonished, and moved. It was the first time he had ever said anything like that. He went on:

"My mother always wanted me to be something like a doctor or a lawyer. Maybe I'd a made a good lawyer. I talk so much. I guess I got that from my father. I'm really kinda shy. Didn't get as much schooling as I wanted to. But common sense is just as good. My parents did what they could for me and my brother, scuffling down in Kentucky where things was hard. I bought 'em a new house and some furniture and two cars. I think they're proud of me now, no matter what people say. I'm glad I could get 'em out of a rut."

"Everybody will be proud of you if you will just give them a chance. Americans, Africans, everybody. Look how the British are treating you."

"Yeh, they sure are nice to me, all right. Wonder what makes 'em so nice? Have they ever been in any big wars?"

I thought back to the awful bombings in Britain during the Second World War. He was not born at the time. "Yes, several," I said.

Two mornings before the fight Angelo telephoned me: "The champ wants you at a press conference at ten this morning. He says he's going to say something you'll like to hear."

"I'll be there," I said. The conference would be at Isow's, a kosher restaurant where he took his meals. I went to Muhammad's room first.

"Here's what I'm going to say," he said. "Read it and tell me what you think."

It was a note, scribbled in red ink, and it began by thanking everyone from the restaurant chef to the prime minister for his "kindness and understanding." Halfway through, Muhammad got to the point: "When I was campaigning for the championship, I said things and did things not becoming of a champion. But I'm champion now. And today I'm measuring my words. I'm measuring my deeds. I'm measuring my thoughts. By the help of the Honorable Elijah Muhammad, this is the new Muhammad Ali. And last, I want to mention something that is nearest to me—the country in which I was born. . . ."

("Wouldn't just 'my country' be better?" I asked. "No," he said, "Elijah Muhammad would like it better the way it is.")

". . . I thank the President of the United States and the officials of the government. And I thank my draft board for letting me come here to defend the title. Regardless of the right or wrong back there, that is where I was born. That is where I'm going to return."

"Beautiful, brother," I said.

Minutes later, dressed in a black silk lounge suit, Muhammad Ali sparkled with confidence and charm as he faced the battery of microphones and reporters. By now I was sure that what he would say came from an impulsive, well-intentioned heart. But I wasn't listening as he spoke. I stood in the back of the room, wondering whether his new high resolve could last.

It was possible, I decided. There would be times when he could, under the pressure of hostile questions, forget and say or do something hopelessly wrong. I decided to wait and see.

Three months is not the longest of trials, but it is a summer's worth at least and a time during which Muhammad Ali managed absolutely to keep his cool, despite some easy chances to lose it. The fight with Brian London had had problems. The press welcomed the champion back to England courteously, even warmly. But as the fight drew nearer and public interest in it kept dropping, reporters tried to stir things up by needling Muhammad. Muhammad merely guzzled down more orange juice and sparred even less. At a press conference, a reporter suggested to him that he looked fat and undertrained. Instead of answering, Muhammad turned casually to me.

"Where'd you get that foxy suit you got on, boss?"

"At my London tailor," I said.

"Well, call him up and tell him I want six just like it— all dark and conservative." Later, in Savile Row, he selected the materials in less than ten minutes. "And make me a vest for each one. I'm a gentleman now. I've got to look like one," he instructed the happy tailor.


As matters turned out, of course, the fight answered a number of criticisms about how well Muhammad Ali had trained and how hard he could hit. On his way into the ring, he had been serenaded with boos. The catcalls had continued as he prayed briefly to Allah before the bell. But when he jogged around the ring, as attendants helped poor London off the canvas, there were only cheers.

Back at the hotel he preened before the mirror in his

new tailored suit. "Well, you changed their song real quick," I said.

"Yep, boss, I picked up a lot of new fans tonight. I won't be getting no more boos 'til I get back where I was born."

"You face isn't even marked."

"Nope. Can't afford marks. The public likes pretty gentlemen fighters. So it looks like Muhammad has to stay pretty and be a gentleman forever and ever."

Someone laughed, but the champion seemed dead serious. And he just might do it, I decided. For, at last, he seemed fully aware of the kind of behavior that brings respect. Already a brilliant fighter, there was hope now that he might become a champion everyone could look up to. If only those back where he was born extended their patience, they would help buoy that hope. From where I had watched and listened, it all seemed so worthwhile.

*Muhammad Ali went on to successfully defend his title against Brian London, Karl Mildenberger, Cleveland Williams, Ernie Terrel and Zora Folley. And now, a calm seemed to be taking over. There were fewer and fewer poems speaking out his greatness. Then, settling in as a Muslim minister, he began taking his religious duties most seriously. He divorced his first wife, Sonji, because she would not abide by the rules of the Black Muslim faith.*

*On April 28, 1967, he was ordered to Houston, Texas, for induction into the Army. He reported, but when he was asked to take the "one step forward," he refused. His faith forbade him from fighting wars "not declared by Allah." For this he was given the maximum penalty: five years in jail and a ten-thousand-dollar fine. Then, almost too quickly, he was stripped of his title. The New York State Athletic Commission revoked his license. The Justice Department picked up his passport, preventing him from practicing his profession in some other country.*

*During Muhammad Ali's enforced retirement his main source of income came from college lectures—he averaged seventy-five appearances a year. He is also a sizable holder in the Florida-based Champburger chain. He seems to have found happiness with Belinda Boyd, his new wife, who grew up in the Black Muslim movement. They have two small children and make their home in Philadelphia.*

*Muhammad Ali was permitted to fight in America once again in October, 1970, when he defeated Jerry Quarry in Atlanta in three rounds. In December, 1970, he fought Oscar Bonavena in New York, defeating him in fourteen rounds. At this writing he is preparing for a title bout with Joe Frazier in which he will seek to regain the title he never lost.*

*To me, and to many sports fans around the world, Muhammad Ali has always been the champion. No fighter withstood his fire. His crown was wrested by a primitive law that sets man upon man for death. He refused that law for what he felt was a higher one. I saw him recently. He is a little heavier and a lot quieter. He has indeed become a gentleman. What's more, he looks like one.*

# 5. Stokely Carmichael

MAY, 1967

*Stokely Carmichael was propelled to the center of the black revolution by racism—both black and white. An early admirer of Martin Luther King and nonviolence, he finally turned, his patience exhausted, on white society. It was his strident call for Black Power that set off a chain reaction hardly to be equaled in our time. At twenty-five, as leader of the Student Nonviolent Coordinating Committee (SNCC or Snick), he was lionized, damned and discussed more than any other black leader in the civil rights movement. The more conservative blacks were disturbed by him, although he was an outgrowth of a militant mood, rather than the creator of it.*

*Stokely addressed his audiences with a biting directness which some found inspiring, but which others felt was irresponsible and divisive. He flailed away with one angry message after another: "Our grandfathers and our great-grandfathers had to run, run, run!" he cried to a West Coast audience. "My generation has run out of breath. We just ain't running no more!" To a surging crowd of anti-Vietnam demonstrators he cried, "Hell, no, we won't go!" When he spoke in Nashville, the blacks rioted. The*

*Tennessee House of Representatives called for his depor-*
*tation. But he roared on across the country, undaunted,*
*from San Francisco to Harlem, fanning the flames of dis-*
*content. But for all the fire and brimstone, he had a boy-*
*ish charm that eventually got to you.*

*I traveled with him for three months. In quieter mo-*
*ments, on a plane late at night, or in a hotel room, he*
*sometimes collapsed into the weary young man that he*
*really was—angry, confused and aware that his role was*
*steadily growing beyond his experience. "I don't know*
*where I'm headed," he confessed sleepily one night. "I'd*
*like to go away and think things over for a while, or maybe*
*go back to school. Perhaps I've gone as far as I can at this*
*point." In retrospect I think he may have been groping for*
*my advice, but I offered him none. We lay in silence for*
*a while, dozing off. "Whatever happens," he went on,*
*"we've stirred the consciousness of black people. We've*
*got the black community on the path to complete libera-*
*tion." Two weeks later, before the article which follows*
*was published, he resigned his post with SNCC.*

*T*he guards had fanned out around the platform at Watts, feet planted apart, arms folded, eyes cut-
ting into the jubilant crowd. I crouched between two of
the guards, my back against the platform. More than
4,000 Negroes and a few whites had gathered. Signs with

protest slogans jabbed the hot air. The stern image of Malcolm X, stenciled on yellow sweatshirts, wriggled over the bosoms of several girls as they leaped and screamed like cheerleaders. This crowd was tailor-made for Stokely Carmichael. All they wanted was just plain down-home, up-tight, nitty-gritty, git-with-it talk.

"All right! All right! Cool it!" a voice boomed over the loudspeaker. "Before Brother Stokely says a word, all white newsmen, and black newsmen with *one-day contracts* from the white press, and all TV men, move to the back of the crowd! Move quickly! We don't want to have to move you!" The orders were promptly obeyed. A big black man, pushing his luck as a lone dissenter, bawled out at the guards, "You damned incendiaries! You goddamned . . ." Before he could repeat his cry, he was strong-armed off the field.

First Stokely made a modest pitch for money. When the donations came in faster than the small buckets could hold them, Cliff Vaughs, a Snick worker, grabbed an old leather satchel off the platform. When he opened it, his jaw dropped and he quickly snapped the bag shut. "That damn thing is full of equalizers," he whispered to me.

Stokely made his stock speech, which I had heard many times—a fiery cry for Black Power and a vitriolic condemnation of the war in Vietnam. ("McNamara is trying to thin us out. Calls it 'black urban removal.' Well, I've got news for Mister Mac. Ain't no Vietcong ever called me nigger . . . and if I'm going to do any fighting it's gonna be right here at home. We will not fight in Vietnam and run in Georgia!")

On the way out, groups of boys and girls rushed his car. Stokely waved at them. "Those kids will be calling me Uncle Tom in a few years," he said. "People think *I'm* militant. Wait until those kids grow up! There are young cats around here who make me look like a dove of peace."

I nodded. We had seen some of those "young cats" the night before in the back room of an old building just outside Watts. Hard times and distrust marked their faces. Members of various militant organizations, they had come to discuss plans for protecting Stokely during the speech at Watts. He hadn't asked for protection, but a brother explained why he was getting it: "It's kind of voluntarily compulsive-like. We don't want another Malcolm X deal here in Watts." Tommy Jacquette, tall and brooding—a young Watts nationalist leader who was Stokely's self-appointed bodyguard—had stood in the back, eying everyone suspiciously. The planning session, chaired by Ron Karenga, leader of the nationalist group US, had got off to a sullen start with each faction sniping at the others.

"You brothers don't seem too happy with the way security is shaping up," Karenga said. A big fellow sitting to one side of the room cut in: "Trouble is, you jokers are tryin' to run things *your* way." At the touch of Karenga's knee, a young tough beside him stood up. "Bastard!" he snarled. "Call one of us a joker again and I'll knock your goddamned teeth down your throat!" The big fellow chose silence. Then the door opened and the Sons of

Watts, more veterans of the 1965 riots, filed in. About twenty of them lined up against one wall.

"We're discussing security, brothers," Karenga explained. "Got anything to say?" I glanced at Stokely. His eyes played on the ceiling.

"Carmichael's going to be in Watts," the Sons' leader said. "Nobody knows Watts better than us. And we don't intend to be out in left field directing traffic. We're gonna be where the action is or we ain't gonna be there at all. We can't protect the brother unless we're in close."

The argument got hotter. Finally Stokely spoke up, softly, persuasively: "Brothers, let's not argue among ourselves. The leaders of each group should get together, outside this room, and decide how each group will participate." Things cooled off a little.

Later, as we drove into downtown Los Angeles, I said, "Rough session." Stokely nodded: "Now, those are the brothers the crackers had better start worrying about." He began to laugh, beating the dashboard with his fist. "Lord! Tonight, when those tough-looking brothers strolled in, I started praying to May Charles, my dear worrying mother."

Cool, outwardly imperturbable, Stokely gives the impression he would stroll through Dixie in broad daylight using the Confederate flag for a handkerchief.

In the four months that I traveled with him I marveled at his ability to adjust to any environment. Dressed in bib overalls, he tramped the backlands of Lowndes County, Alabama, urging Negroes, in a Southern-honey drawl, to register and vote. The next week, wearing a tight dark suit and Italian boots, he was in Harlem lining up cats for the cause, using the language they dig most—hip and very cool. A fortnight later, jumping from campuses to intellectual salons, he spoke with eloquence and ease about his cause, quoting Sartre, Camus and Thoreau.

But wherever he went, Stokely was never very far from his identification with Snick—the Student Nonviolent Coordinating Committee. As its chairman for the past year and a field organizer for five previous years, he has been shaped by Snick's bitter fight for its cause.

Snick, founded in 1960, got its start as an activist organization the next summer when a vanguard of thirteen members, most of them Southern college students, spread through the Deep South with the bold idea of breaking the code that since emancipation had sent thousands of Negroes to their deaths simply because they had attempted to vote. The group bedded down in sharecroppers' shacks, scrounged for food and clothing and went to work organizing local Negroes. Snick grew rapidly, and by 1964 there were nearly 1,000 members and volunteers working in the dangerous black belt of the South.

They were not fearless, storybook heroes. The girls screamed when they were beaten. The boys yelled and writhed when the special handcuffs—"wrist-breakers"—were clamped on and the protruding screws dug into their veins. They kept singing because singing was sometimes their only link with sanity. The experience left Stokely, who joined Snick at its founding, a complex young rebel. By the time he was twenty-two he had acquired an ulcer and was close to a nervous breakdown.

Today the official Snick organization numbers only 100 —with hundreds of other nonpaid volunteers and sympathizers who send money and help with fund-raising campaigns. The 100 are paid salaries of $20 a week, which they seldom collect. They are still committed to non-violence—*as a tactical approach.* But, as Stokely points out, "Our organization feels that any man has the right to physically protect his life and his home." At Atlanta headquarters the last few months, while Stokely has been in headlines, the staff has been working on the political organizing they expect to accomplish in the Deep South this summer.

It is this basic field work to which Stokely is anxious to return now that he has given up Snick's chairmanship. Long before he announced that decision, he talked about the doubts he had of his leadership role. We were in the home of his friend and adviser Professor Charles V. Hamilton, chairman of the political science department at Lincoln University, located near Oxford, Pennsylvania. "I'm an *organizer,*" Stokely said. "I want to go back to what I can do best. I'm too young for this job. I don't know enough about the outside world. I need time to read, learn, reflect. I think, perhaps, that more than anything else I'd like to be a college professor."

Stokely's ulcer was acting up and he sipped a glass of

milk. "Those black kids," he said gesturing toward students crossing the campus outside the window, "they'll be fighting for a different power, not the kind the Irish and Italian immigrants got. And they'll probably get what they want—although we won't be around to see it. . . . But someone must first teach them to respect themselves, to sit still and listen—otherwise they won't pull off a political revolution."

Stokely was weary after the drive from New York to Oxford, part of which we had made in a snow storm, and he turned from the window and stretched out on the floor. That afternoon I had seen a flash of the irrepressible humor that helps him keep his balance. Near Oxford the car had skidded and got stuck in a drift. Stokely gunned the motor, but the wheels just spun in their tracks. We tried rocking the car free several times. But we were in good and deep. Finally he cut the motor and we sat there for a few moments. Suddenly the incongruity of the situation struck him. He raised his arms and, shaking both fists violently, shouted, "Black Power! Black Power!"

Now, sprawled on Hamilton's living-room rug, Stokely began a rambling recollection of the time in 1961 when he was thrown into a crowded cell at the state farm prison near Parchman, Mississippi: "They did everything to us there but lynch us. We're singing one night and in comes this beloved cracker. 'Y'all niggers stop that damn noise or I'm gonna fix you.' We keep right on. Then he says, 'Take the black bastards' blankets!' They grab Hank Thomas's first, but he holds on like a leech. They finally

shake him off. The cracker points at me. 'You goddamned nigger! I'm gonna see to it that you never get outta here.' Meanwhile, they're clamping wrist-breakers on Freddie Leonard. They're hurting that cat so bad he's twisting around on the floor like a snake. The cracker says to him, 'You tryin' to hit me, nigger?' 'Oh, no,' says Freddie, 'I'm just waiting for you to break my arm.' You should have seen that *white man's face!* He was so shook up he just stood there snarling like an animal. All this time we kept singing, *'I'm gonna tell God how you treat me.'* I was leading the singing, so the cracker hollered, 'Git that nigger's mattress!' They bumped me against the floor several times, but I held on. Finally, the old guy gave up. 'Throw him back in the cell!' he shouted. Then he went out the door cussing like hell. We kept singing all night."

Stokely fell silent and his mood changed. He began to describe a march back in 1964, and as he spoke we could feel the billies cracking against the head of John Lewis, Stokely's predecessor as Snick chairman. "As he goes down time and time again, he's moaning, 'I love you. I love you.' And they pick him up again. *Bam! Smack! Bam!* 'You black son-of-a-bitch!' And John, the true believer in nonviolence, sinks half-conscious to the pavement. Now we're retreating. They're coming after us with cattle prods and dogs. 'They've come far enough, baby! Open up.' *Crack! Bam! Pow!* The crackers begin to scatter. 'Shoot out the street lights!' *Bang! Bang!* A big Army captain is telling them to put on the spotlight. 'Shut that damn light off!' A brother zings a burst past the captain's ankles.

The captain hollers, 'Order changed! Ree-treat! These niggers have gone loco! Ree-treat! Ree-treat!' " We laughed ourselves sick as Stokely rolled back and forth screaming "Ree-treat!"

Not until he began recounting the fatal church bombings in Birmingham, Alabama, in 1963, and the murders the next summer near Philadelphia, Mississippi, of the three civil rights workers, Chaney, Schwerner and Goodman, did a quiet come to the room. Stokely recalled how in Montgomery he had broken after seeing a pregnant black woman knocked head over heels by water jetting from a fire hose, and other men and women being trampled by police horses. "Suddenly," he said, rubbing his eyelids, "everything blurred. I started screaming and I didn't stop until they got me to the airport. That day I knew I could never be hit again without hitting back."

Stokely was "born smart" in Trinidad on June 29, 1941, and brought to Harlem when he was eleven. Later, when his family moved to the Bronx, he became the sole Negro member of the Morris Park Dukes, a neighborhood gang.

Things changed quickly when he was accepted at the Bronx High School of Science, which takes only bright kids: "I broke from the Dukes. They were reading funnies while I was trying to dig Darwin and Marx. But I found myself in another kind of bag at Bronx Science. All those rich kids with their maids and chauffeurs began getting their kicks out of me. 'You're different,' they'd say.

"I began making the Village scene and parties down on Park Avenue. I felt strange every time a black maid handed me something. My mother, May Charles, was also a maid, making thirty bucks a week.

"I read a lot, but I wasn't hip about many things. In 1960, when I first heard about the Negroes sitting-in at lunch counters down South, I thought they were just a bunch of publicity hounds. But one night when I saw those kids on TV, getting back up on the lunch-counter stools after being knocked off them, sugar in their eyes, catsup in their hair—well, something happened to me. Suddenly I was burning. Then I started picketing all over the place with a bunch of kids from CORE.

"After a few beatings on those picket lines, I realized that it was either them or me. I preferred me." Several white schools offered him scholarships, but Stokely went to Howard University in Washington, D.C. "It was a natural. It was black. I could keep in touch with the movement there."

When Stokely was a freshman, he was on his way to his first Freedom Ride to challenge segregated interstate travel. May Charles Carmichael says he just phoned from school one evening and told her he was going to Mississippi to join the Riders.

" 'Don't worry, Mom,' he told me. 'I'm going to jail, but you must be proud of me and not ashamed.' I sat by the radio all that night worrying. In a few days I heard that he had been arrested and taken to prison, and then everybody was calling up, asking, 'Is that your boy

Stokely they've got down there?' And I would say, 'Yes, that's my boy and I'm so proud of him I don't know what to do!'

"Sometimes now," says May Charles, "I think of him defying anyone for what he believes and I can't figure him out. When he was little, all the kids bullied him. Why, he was even scared of cats! Then, when he found out what he wanted to do, I asked him, 'Son, are you trying to be a big shot or a politician or something like that?' I've never seen him madder. 'I've got one son,' I told him. 'Let other Negroes give of theirs for a while.' He shot right back, 'What's all this religious stuff you taught me about Abraham sacrificing his son? If you really believe that, you shouldn't mind sacrificing yours.' "

Ever since Stokely first raised the cry of Black Power, he has had his detractors among the nationally known—and well-respected—Negro leaders. They have viewed his Black Power philosophy and antiwar chanting with consternation, asserting he does more to damage the cause than to help it. An exception among the moderates is Martin Luther King, for whom Stokely has great respect. Dr. King has called Black Power a "confusing" phrase, but he has never actually denounced it and he has joined with Stokely in linking the Vietnam protest to the civil rights issue.

Roy Wilkins of the N.A.A.C.P. says, "No matter how endlessly they try to explain Black Power, the term means antiwhite. . . . It has to mean going it alone. It has to mean separatism. . . . This offers a disadvantaged minority little except the chance to shrivel and die."

I discussed the term—and Stokely—with Whitney Young of the National Urban League at that organization's well-appointed offices in midtown Manhattan. Whitney, a fine-looking, robust man in his early forties, smiled when I broached the subject. "Well," he said, "Stokely didn't really make the backlash they're all talking about. He just gave them an excuse to come out publicly where they had been hesitant otherwise. But there is no dignity in the withdrawal from society that Stokely preaches. He gives too many Negroes a chance to escape responsibility. We'll have to work hard for what we get. It's better for a black man to reach in his pocket and find a dollar instead of a hole."

The next morning I went to Harlem to talk with Floyd McKissick of CORE in his cluttered little third-floor headquarters. What Floyd says about Stokely isn't much different from what Stokely says about himself, for their philosophy is practically the same. Floyd defends the concept of Black Power strenuously. "It's a drive to unite the black man in America in a gigantic effort to erase the causes of alienation, despair and hopelessness," he said. "It's got to be good if the white man is against it."

Stokely has heard so often the charge he is preaching violence that he meets it with a weary shrug: "I'm not advocating violence. I'm just telling the white man he's beat my head enough. I won't take any more. White

Power makes the laws and White Power, in the form of white cops with guns and night sticks, enforces those laws. The white press equates Black Power—the slogan—with racism and separatism, and gives headlines to black leaders, like Wilkins and Young, who attack it. The stories fail to report the productive dialogue taking place in the black community or in the white religious and intellectual areas. As for separatism, what are they talking about? We have no *choice*." He knifed the air with his finger: "They separated us a long time ago. And they sure intend to keep it that way."

He grinned sardonically. "The white man says, 'Work hard, nigger, and you'll overcome.' Well, if that were true, the black man would be the richest man in the world. My old man believed in this work-and-overcome stuff. He was religious, never lied, never cheated or stole. He did carpentry all day and drove taxis all night. They robbed him right and left. May Charles had to bribe an official with fifty bucks and a bottle of perfume to get him into the union. *He didn't know.* 'See,' he said, 'have patience and things will come to you.' The next thing that came to that poor black man was death—from working too hard. And he was only in his forties."

I finally asked Stokely, "what do you *really* mean by Black Power?"

"I've given up trying to explain it," he said. "The whites never really listen when I do, anyway."

"But I'm not white and I'm listening," I insisted.

"*For the last time*," he said, "Black Power means black

people coming together to form a political force and either electing representatives or forcing their representatives to speak their needs. It's an economic and physical bloc that can exercise its strength in the black community instead of letting the job go to the Democratic or Republican parties or a white-controlled black man set up as a puppet to represent black people. *We* pick the brother and make sure he fulfills *our* needs. Black Power doesn't mean antiwhite, violence, separatism or any other racist things the press says it means. It's saying, 'Look, buddy, we're not laying a vote on you unless you lay so many schools, hospitals, playgrounds and jobs on us.'"

Not long after Stokely had made his controversial appearance at the giant antiwar rally at the United Nations, I dropped in on him one night at his home in the Bronx. He was very tired.

"I don't want personal admiration," he said. "The movement is the important thing. It must live after I'm gone. That was the second tragedy of Malcolm X's death. There was no movement left to carry on."

"You don't expect to go the way he did, do you?"

"The crackers will get me before the summer's over. I'm sure of that. But I'm not worried. There are too many others who believe as I do. I'm expendable."

"You were pretty rough with McNamara, Rusk and Johnson in your speech," I said.

"They deserved every bit of it. My words for them don't start to match the criminal acts they perpetrate against the Vietnamese people. How can McNamara deny racism when proportionately more black boys are dying every day in his stinking war? To black people all over, the U.S. military in Vietnam is international white supremacy. Anyone who thinks otherwise is a victim of U.S. brainwashing."

"Aren't you confusing civil rights issues with the issues for peace?"

"I support Dr. King's theories here," Stokely said. "The people who support the war in Vietnam are the same ones who keep their foot on the black man's neck in this country. Bigotry and death over here is no different from bigotry and death over there."

"What about the Negro soldiers who feel they are fighting for a stake in this country?"

"Our stake will come from the struggle against white supremacy here at home. I'd rather die fighting here tomorrow than live twenty years fighting over there. Why should I go help the white man kill other dark people while he's still killing us here at home?"

I couldn't help thinking about my son who is serving as a tank gunner in Vietnam. A week before, he had received the Purple Heart; his buddy was killed by a sniper. "I now have my fifth kill, dad," he wrote with a kind of frozen passion. "We got the bastard sniper later that afternoon." This from a boy who once said he would never be able to kill. Now, glancing at Stokely, I wondered which boy was giving himself to a better cause. There was no immediate answer. But in the face of death, which was so possible for both of them, I think Stokely would surely be more certain of why he was about to die.

Stokely said, "Remember, we fought three hundred years of American Negro history in a year and a half—organizing, bleeding, starving and educating at the same time. We gave a nation hope. If there is a future for us, we had better face it with hard political lines."

He rubbed his eyes. "Americans cannot face reality. They won't admit to their racism. But it was racism that got me involved in this movement—not love. Maybe we shouldn't be ashamed of hate. Like love, it's a human emotion even if it has a dangerous energy.

"I suppose it's pride, more than color, that binds me to my race. And I'm learning that the concern for blackness is necessary, but the concern has to go further than *that* to reach anyone who needs it.

"Mississippi taught me that one's life isn't too much to give to help rid a nation of fascists. Camus says, 'In a revolutionary period it is always the best who die. The law of sacrifice leaves the last word to the cowards and the timorous, since the others have lost it by giving the best of themselves.' I dig Camus," he said, smiling. Then he stood up, kissed May Charles good night and went off to bed.


*Today Stokely Carmichael still makes occasional forays into the limelight, but he spends much of his time out of the public eye in Conakry, Guinea, where he lives with his wife, the singer Miriam Makeba.*

# 6. The Fontenelle Family

MARCH, 1968

*T*he coming of winter this year was a bad time for Norman Fontenelle. When I first saw him, he had just been laid off from his part-time job as a railway section hand. There was almost no money left, or food. None of his kids had winter coats, and if it turned much colder, they wouldn't be able to go to school. "It's awful," he said, squinting through eyes that are always bloodshot. "I've got ten mouths to feed here and there ain't enough in that icebox to even fill the baby's stomach. What can I do? The black man gets the walking papers first. And he's the last to be called back. The white man does all the hirin' and firin'. Not much to do about it. I don't have a education so I can't get anything better. That's why I hang onto this job. But after working eleven years for a company, you'd think they'd take you on steady."

Norman Fontenelle is a quiet, short, powerfully built man, but defeat is hanging off him. He came to Harlem fifteen years ago, with big plans, from St. Lucia in the British West Indies. "It's a pretty place," he said wistfully. "I'd like to take my whole family there—away from

113

this miserable damn place." Four flights up in an old brick building on Eighth Avenue the Fontenelles exist as best they can. There's Norman, 38, and Bessie, 39, his wife; Phillip, 15; Roseanna, 14; Norman, Jr., 13; Riel, 12; Lette, 9; Kenneth, 8; Ellen, 5, and Richard, 3. And a bad-tempered dog named Toe-boy and a cat, who are there really to keep the roaches and the rats in check. Many Harlem families keep pets for the same reason. Norman says bitterly, "The rent's seventy dollars a month and the whole building's crawling with roaches and rats. The plaster is falling down. It ain't fit for dogs. But what can you do? My wife's always trying to get into one of those projects, but they won't let us in until I get a steady job. So we're always finding ourselves right where we started—nowhere." The Fontenelles once also had gold-fish. One morning when I got there, Little Richard was pointing at the bowl on the mantel. The heat had gone off the night before and three fish were floating on the surface, dead from the cold. "Fishies dead, fishies dead," he kept mumbling.

Bessie Fontenelle appears to be a strong woman, especially in the early part of the day, when she looks younger than thirty-nine. As the day wears on, she seems to age with it. By nightfall she has crumpled into herself. "All this needing and wanting is about to drive me crazy," she said to me one evening. "Now I've got double trouble. My husband is a good man, but every time they fire him or lay him off, he takes it out on me and the kids. He gets his little bottle and starts nipping. By the time he nips

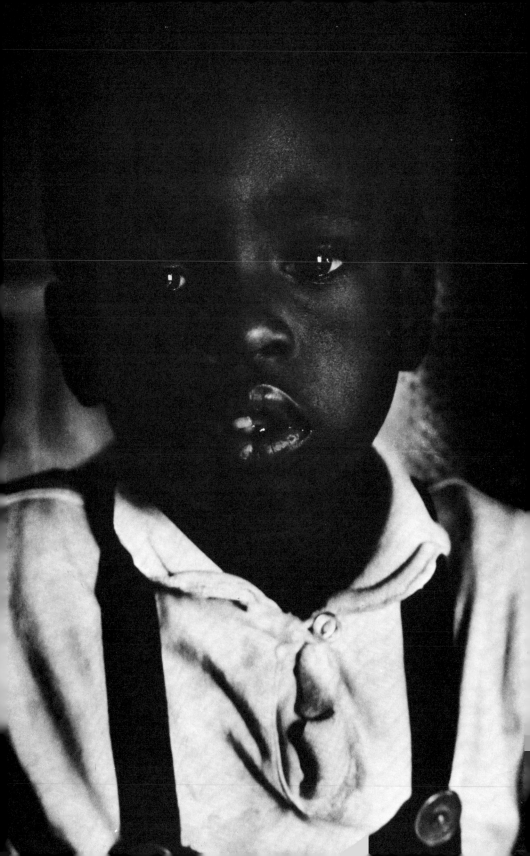

to the bottom, he's mad with the whole world. Then the kids and I get it, especially Norman, Jr. Those two don't get along at all. That boy keeps telling him he'll kill him if he keeps beating up on me. I wouldn't be surprised someday if he'll just up and do it."

Bessie tries to give warmth to his home, but it remains a prison of endless filth, cluttered with rags and broken furniture. Her touch shows in the shapeless, soiled curtains; the dime-store paintings on the walls; the shredded scatter rugs covering the cracked linoleum; the wax flowers and outdated magazines. It is a losing battle.

I have yet to see all the Fontenelles sitting down and eating together. One of the kids will cry his hunger and Bessie will scrounge up a sandwich of some kind. Norman, Jr., seems to exist on tiny 7-cent sweet-potato pies from the grocery store. Little Richard was eating a raw potato one day. Sometimes four of the younger kids hungrily share one apple. But even if there was enough food for regular meals, the kitchen table is too small to accommodate all ten of them at once.


Lette came into the room crying. Norman, Jr., had thumped her on the head. Bessie dropped her head into her hands: "Oh, God, if it ain't one thing, it's another." Little Richard joined in the crying. His swollen lips were cracked and bleeding. "Oh, God, oh, God," Bessie said. She put on some ointment. Then, weary and distraught, she lay down and began to moan. Kenneth came in from the kitchen and sat down beside her. "You all right, Momma?" he asked. "You all right?"

Norman, Jr., was holding a big roll of masking tape. "Look, Momma, what I got." He stripped a long piece off and cut it up with a paring knife. Then he began covering a hole in the wall by his bed.

"Is that to keep out the rats?" I asked.

"Naw," he said. "They eat right through this stuff. This is to keep out the wind."

I caught up with Mrs. Fontenelle and four of her kids at the antipoverty office. She was looking for help and wanted anyway to make some complaints about the rats and the roaches and the garbage and the broken windows and the heat going off. "The landlord looks and promises, but nothing happens. But just let us miss that seventy-dollar rent one month and he's threatening to put us in the street." Bob Haggins, the board director, sat in his overcoat and listened to her. The poverty office had also been without heat for the last three days. He asked her where she came from. "North Carolina," Bessie said. "I heard all about the big factories that were going up in the cities. I didn't know it would be like this."

"You have to keep faith," Haggins told her and said he would try to get Norman into some kind of job training that would pay him $2 an hour.

Norman, Jr., and Kenneth lay on their sheetless bunks, fully clothed and under blankets, fighting the cold and their homework. Roseanna had given in momentarily to a comic book. Lette had been excused from studying. Her glasses were broken. Welfare had promised her a new pair, but that had been two weeks before. Now she was having dizzy spells when she tried to read. It is Bessie who insists on homework. "Seems the most important thing now is to try to get them some kind of education," she said to me. "That's why I make them keep working. If just one of these kids can make it in some way, I'll be thankful." The way the kids keep their books so neatly stacked in all the rubble is amazing. In the quieter moments, the older ones help the others with their lessons. At such times the house seems to be filled with love.

Roseanna sat with her head buried in her hands, barefoot, with a black raincoat buttoned against the cold. She wouldn't talk to me. I walked past her into the kitchen. "Want to know what's the matter with Rosie?" Kenneth whispered. "Momma whipped her for staying out all night last night." I asked Rosie about it. "Us kids don't have any place to go. That particular night we were at a girl friend's house, dancing and having fun. It got so late we were all afraid to go home, so we just hung out until morning." Later three of Rosie's friends—two boys and a girl—came by. They sat in the semidarkness of Rosie's room on a bundle of rags and the unmade bed, their coats on, hardly saying anything to one another, sharing a single cigarette. It was as though they had

come not to visit but to escape the weather and share each other's misery.


Bessie Fontenelle reached over and straightened a picture of Christ that hangs over the baby's crib. I asked her if they were a religious family. Just as she was about to answer, Ellen screamed. Toe-boy had nipped her toe. Bessie sent the dog scurrying with a well-aimed kick. "Well, I guess we are—at least we used to be. We just don't go to church any more. I have to be truthful. It's hard keeping faith in something when everything's going so bad for you. I teach the kids their prayers, and that's the best I can do."


It was snowing when I left, and the flakes were swirling down through an open skylight and piling up in a hallway by their door. On the street below I came up on Norman, Jr., peering through the window of a fish-and-chips joint. "Want some chips?" he asked hopefully. I told him I'd love some. So we went in and filled our stomachs with greasy fried potatoes and fish. He is a strange mixture. In his talk there is a defiance for whites—the white policeman, the white butcher, the white grocery clerk. His eyes have the hard glint of older black men in Harlem. At thirteen he is already primed for some kind of action. He is aggressive, determined and powerfully built for his age. But his hostility is balanced by an over-

whelming tenderness at times. He will suddenly lift little
Richard off the floor and smother him with kisses. At times
he stands beside his mother, affectionately fingering her
earrings. "You're pretty, Momma, real pretty," he'll say
without smiling.

On another day, Rosie lured me into the fish-and-
chips place. Through the steamy window, Lette spotted
us eating and came in to join us. I asked Lette what she
would like and she pointed to the greasy potatoes. "No
fish or chicken?" I asked. Her eyes lit up. "Chicken? That's
too much money, ain't it?" I told her to order chicken.

Each day Bessie seems to sink into deeper despair. She
complains constantly about the filth and the falling plaster. "I could clean this place every hour and it would still
look the same. There's no place to put anything. I stay
tired all the time. Over at the hospital they say it's my
nerves. They want to open my throat and operate for
some reason. Sometimes I feel like jumping out the window. But there's the kids to look after."

Two children of the family do not live at home. "My
oldest girl, Diana, is graduating from nursing school up
in Massachusetts this year," Bessie said. "She'll make it."
Harry, twenty, is confined as a narcotics addict at Brentwood, twenty-five miles east of Harlem, in New York's
Pilgrim State Hospital. "He got on dope he was fifteen,"

Bessie said. "I did everything I could—even took him to the police. But once he was hung up, there was nothing to do. To protect the other kids I finally had to throw him out of the house when he was about eighteen." Brentwood is $4.50 in railway fare, too much; so none of the family has visited Harry in the six months he's been there. On a Sunday morning I drove Norman, Sr., and Bessie up to see him. The first moments of the meeting were awkward.

"How's all the kids?" Harry asked.

"They're all fine and send you their love," said Bessie.

"They treating you all right?" asked Norman.

"Everything's okay. I should be out in another seven months."

"You're fat."

"Think so? They got any heat in the house for you this year?"

"Oh, yes," Bessie cut in. "Everything's just going fine at home." I swallowed the lie heavily. Then Bessie got to what was really on her mind. "I hope you come out good and clean, Harry. You've had enough trouble already."

"Oh, I'll be straight. Everything'll be straight, Mom."

"I hope to God you never touch the stuff again."

His answer stunned all three of us. "Well, I don't know —I can't say for sure I'll never go back on it. You see, I wasn't on heroin, just on cocaine—which isn't so bad."

Suddenly Harry saw how much his words had hurt Bessie. He choked out a sob and covered his face.

There was no heat in the apartment. There hadn't been any the night before. The ten of them had slept huddled together on mattresses in the kitchen with the oven going all night. Bessie and the children were still there when I arrived in the morning. They were eating warmed-over fish for breakfast. Fish—just on the edge of spoiling—is a staple for them. It is cheaper than anything else. That night they were planning Thanksgiving dinner, their most luxurious meal in months: sausage and eggs.

"How's it going?" I asked one morning.

"Not good at all," said Norman.

"Any hope for going back to work?"

"I was out for the shape-up every day this week." He rubbed his head. "Any other man would have been gone long time ago. A lot of these guys up here do. But I can't leave. All I want to be is a man," he said finally.

I found Norman, Jr., standing around on the street corner, warming himself over a garbage-can fire. The smell of snow was in the air. The boy wore tennis shoes and a light windbreaker, the heaviest coat he owned. I asked him what he was doing out so late in the cold.

"Poppa put me out," he said, rubbing his hands together over the flame.

"For what?"

"For nothing. He's mad about not having any work, I guess."

I asked him if I could do anything.

"Naw," he answered. "Momma will fix things up. I'll be all right."

Upstairs, I could hear an argument through the door before I knocked. It stopped when I went in, but there was tension in the chilly apartment. Norman, Sr., was slumped in a dark corner. I sat around for nearly half an hour in the uncomfortable stillness. Bessie went with me to the door. She was really down in the dumps. "Things are a little rough here tonight," she said softly. "One of his friends gave him a bottle."

Next afternoon when I arrived, Bessie was lying on her bed, groaning in misery. Little Richard had crawled beneath her arm. Her neck was scratched and swollen. She managed a painful half-smile. "He gave me a going-over last night. My ribs feel like they're broken." She began to cry. "I just can't take it no more. It's too much for anybody to bear." I asked where Norman, Sr., was. In the hospital, she said. "When he got through kicking me, I got up and poured some sugar and honey into a boiling pan of water and let him have it in the face." Why the sugar and honey? "To make it stick and burn for a while."

Norman, Jr., and I went over to the hospital. It was almost impossible to recognize the father. The honey and sugar still coated his neck and face, and his right hand was horribly burned. He sat up on the side of the bed

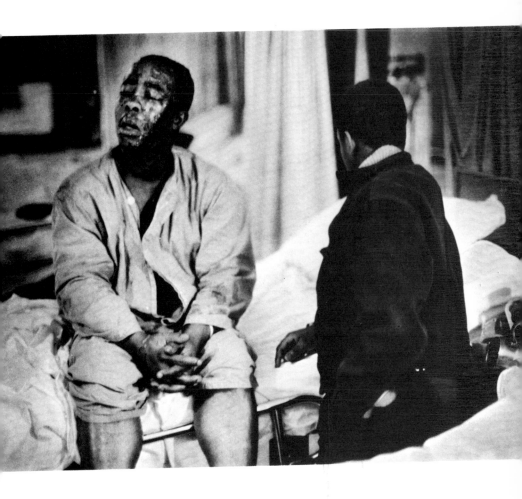

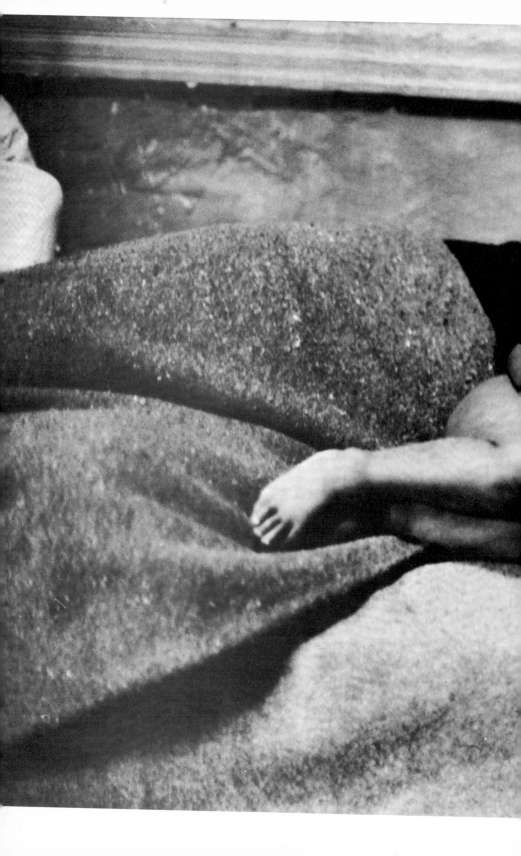

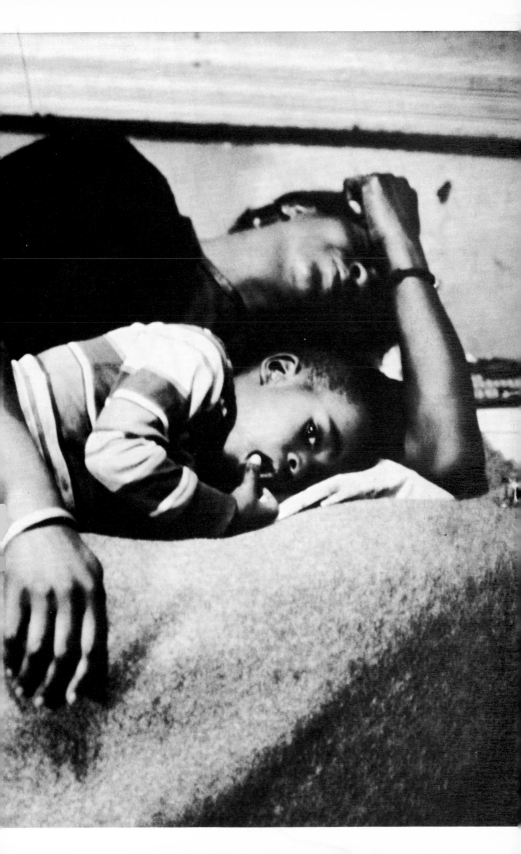

and daubed at his eyes. "I don't know why your mother did it, boy," he said. "I just don't know why." Then he lay back down and lapsed into painful sleep.

Just another one of the thousands of violences that explode in a ghetto every week, I thought as we left. In the heat of summer they pile up and spill into the street. And buildings burn and people are killed and windows are smashed. And the Normans, big and small, dash in to loot what they don't have at home.

Snow was falling again. He headed back toward that cold apartment, and I wondered why they waited for summer.

*After the Fontenelles' story was published, the family was able to move to a comfortable little house in Long Island, with the help of* Life *and contributions from its readers. There was new furniture, a front porch, grass and fresh air, and good schools nearby. Eventually Harry left prison, swearing off dope forever; and Norman was promised a better job. An entirely new world had suddenly raced in upon the Fontenelles and swept them away from the filth and chaos of that Harlem tenement. "It's hard to believe," Norman kept saying. "It's hard to believe." None of them were prouder than Norman, Jr. He led me through the house with his mother in tow. "Look! Look!" he shouted, pointing at the new stove, the sparkling new frigidaire, the washing machine. "Just lookit that! They're all Momma's!" Rosie popped up. "See how clean everything is, no dirty dishes or nothing." The entire family was happy. I was happy for them.*

*Then at three o'clock one morning several months later, fire destroyed the little house, young Kenneth and Norman, Sr. In less than one hour, horror had replaced their happiness.*

*One Christmas Eve later, what remained of the family was back in Harlem, all except Harry, who was once more imprisoned. Norman, Jr., was out of school again. Rosie had taken off on her own. There wasn't much I could say to Bessie Fontenelle as I left them that night. She stood, I remember, at the top of the stairs waving good-by. She finally said what I could not bring myself to say, "Merry Christmas." "And a happy New Year," I called back. Perhaps I shouldn't have touched that family, I thought to myself, as I pulled out of the block.*

# 7. On the Death of
# Martin Luther King, Jr.

APRIL, 1968

*H*ere again was the stench of carnations sweetening the Southern closeness, the white-robed choir singing hymns so familiar to our down-home Sabbath, the black children wondering about the soul of the deceased floating somewhere above them. Here again were the minister and his elders praying to God to take charge of the departed soul. And here was the widow, veiled and beautiful in grief. But in little Ebenezer Baptist Church in Atlanta, packed with its black congregation and a strange scattering of familiar white faces, there was also something hauntingly different. The scratchy, taped voice of the man we sorrowed for echoed off the walls and penetrated our hearts. *". . . and if you're around when I have to meet my day, I don't want a long funeral. And if you get somebody to deliver the eulogy, tell him not to talk too long."* The quiet was heavy as the magnificent revivalist voice of our murdered black leader rolled on. *"I'd like somebody to mention that day that Martin Luther King, Jr., tried to love somebody. . . ."* Standing in the crush along the wall, I closed my eyes, remembering back fifty years, past my sight of the King children, indeed, *through* them, through the odor of camphor and the swishing of fans, to the black funerals of my childhood. Things hadn't got that much better for us. This man, our most celebrated spokesman, lies in a black man's burial ground. *"I want you to be able to say that day that I did try to feed the hungry. I want you to say that I tried to love and serve humanity!"*

In the coffin lay one who had filled us with a sense of hope, a hope that seemed, at this despairing moment, shattered. But in death he had made us know who we are and what we are. He made us know that we were still in a land of oppression and assassins. In spite of the tears in Ebenezer and all over the country, how moved, *really* moved, was the white conscience?

White racists warned Dr. King that they would kill him. They kept their word. And even now, as we sat mourning this tragedy, the spring air over dozens of American cities was darkening to arsonist smoke—the black ghetto's answer to the white racist deed. A distinguished gathering of white government leaders sat beneath the hot roof of Ebenezer. Some had helped Dr. King during his trials. But others hadn't, and most of their soul brothers hadn't cared at all. Over a bonfire in Yazoo City, Mississippi, one night, Martin had answered the black extremist who shouted for blood and fire: "I'm tired of shooting! I'm tired of clubs! I'm tired of killing! I'm tired of war! I'm not going to use violence, no matter who says so!" He had protested the way American whites preferred that he protest—nonviolently. He spent the last dozen years of his life preaching love to men of all colors. And for all this, a man, white like you, blasted a bullet through his neck. And in doing so the madman has just about eliminated the last symbol of peace between us. We must struggle to distinguish between *his* act and *your* conscience.

It is not enough any more when you ask that all whites not be blamed for what one did. You must know how we really feel—before grass takes root over Dr. King's grave. We are angry. All of us. Believe this, no matter what anyone else tells you: you have pushed us to the precipice. Of course we don't blame all of you literally, but we cannot control what is deep in our hearts. The thousands of blacks killed between 1868 and 1968 for just trying to vote, the slayings of little Emmett Till, Medgar Evers, the three civil rights workers Schwerner, Goodman and Chaney, and now Martin Luther King, have not endeared our hearts to you. Too many of us are still unaccounted for in the terror-ridden swamplands of the South.

True, all the burning and looting won't help, but how else could you expect the black ghetto dweller to express his frustration? Could he have called the cop who has given him the back of his hand—and often the end of his club—through all these years? Should he have called the mayor or the White House?

We are wondering a lot of things. Maybe our questions

are expressions of furious emotion, but black men are demanding the answers. Our own tragic experience as second-class citizens in the eyes of the law and the courts leads us to cry: how did one man elude forty policemen assigned to protect Dr. King after blasting a shot over their heads in broad daylight? Where is the killer?

And what will the law do with him when he is caught? Medgar Evers's murderer is only one such assassin still at large. Even punished, Dr. King's killer will remain a symbol of the white attitude toward blacks—unless the redemption goes deeper. A new civil rights bill has passed. That is good, but white America must continue to show the strength of its conscience before we realize its worth.

We have grown to doubt the hopeful songs of our fathers. We wonder if we shall overcome our doubts about your promises. We have grown to lack the patience to wait for God's deliverance. We want a new life. Our youth refuses to sit and wait to share in the affluence that you surround them with. They will cross your line even if it means death. "A man must conquer the fear of death," Dr. King said; "otherwise he is lost already."

No man spoke harder against violence. Yet few men suffered more from it than he. His worship of a higher law got him jailed, stoned and stabbed. He led us into fire hoses, police dogs and police clubs. His only armor was truth and love. Now that he lies dead from a lower law, we begin to wonder if love is enough. Racism still engulfs us. The fires still smolder, and the extremists, black and white, are buying the guns. Everywhere—Army troops stand ready. Our President is warned against going to Atlanta. America is indeed in a state of shock. The white man, stricken, must stay firm in his conscience, and the black man must see that he does. If the death of this great man does not unite us, we are committing ourselves to suicide.

# 8. The Black Panthers and the Police

*FEBRUARY, 1970*

*T*he weapons to be employed: "Rifles, shotguns, 33MM gas guns, 37MM grenade launchers and Thompson sub-machine guns." The assault plans: "Assign two man squad to front with shotgun (solid slugs) and armor piercing rifle to blast armor plate off upper windows. . . . Upper window shields to be shot out, and use 00 buckshot to shoot out all lower windows. Use rifle slugs to try and knock open main front door. . . . Front and back guard lay down fire on the second floor. . . . Assault squad (three men) armed with sub-machine guns approach building from the south. . . . Squad enter building through front broken windows or doors. . . . Two men enter and move left and to right center of ground floor. Fire thirty rounds each up through the second story floor, and reload. . . . The entire building should be flooded with tear gas. The entire upper floor should be covered with intense fire. . . . Assault squad will then proceed upstairs and bring down the wounded and the dead."

The target: the Black Panther Party headquarters on Shattuck Street in Berkeley, California. The task force

("in the event of a disturbance at the Party office"): the Berkeley police.

It was dusk, and I sat in the upstairs kitchen of the Panthers' Berkeley headquarters—the target. Dinner time was near and David Hilliard, the Party's chief of staff, was at the stove stirring a big pot of rabbit stew. The assault plans had fallen into his hands and it was he who had given them to me. David's brother June and Donald Cox, the Party's field marshal, sat observing me from a corner in the poorly lit room. Obviously the three of them were awaiting my reaction. "These plans are incredible," I said. The Hilliard brothers remained silent. Cox grunted and smiled. "The pig is incredible," he answered softly. I didn't ask Hilliard how he got hold of the document, but I surely wanted to. Instead, I asked him if he thought it was authentic. Before he could answer, Cox handed me a newspaper clipping in which Berkeley Police Chief Bruce Baker admitted that the plans were probably the work of his sergeants. But he denied having known anything about them.

"How did it all start between the Panthers and the police?" I asked Hilliard. He tasted the stew and called one of the girls to wash dishes before he answered. "Those pigs have been fucking with us ever since Huey Newton backed down seven of them with an M-1 rifle and a law book." That incident had taken place in 1966 when a policeman had tried to stop Newton, Bobby Seale and several others as they emerged from the Panther office carrying pistols and shotguns. They had just had a lesson in the care and use of guns and ammunition. As Huey argued about their constitutional right to carry weapons, more police arrived and a crowd collected. "That was the day that Huey proved to be the baddest black mother-fucker ever born into history. The pigs kept trying to get the brothers and sisters off the street so they could lay down some shit. But Huey was wise to that. He unlocked the Panther headquarters and let them in so they could watch from a big window." Hilliard stopped suddenly, called another girl and sent her out for some bread. Then he continued stirring all the while.

"The pigs were bugged. One of them asked Huey what he was going to do with the gun. Huey asked him what he was going to do with his gun. 'Because if you try to shoot me or take my gun,' he said, 'I'm gonna unload this M-1 on all of you.' Those cats backed down. And that same morning over a dozen young black cats joined the Black Panthers. Huey did what all those black broth-ers and sisters had wanted to do for a long time. He stood up and told a bunch of cops that he was through having his ass kicked by them. The black brothers on the street got the message. And so did the cops."

"Huey was down with it," Cox cut in. "That law book in his hand was on his side. He knew he had as much right to that M-1 as the cops did. He laid down the important thing for us. Find out what you're doing, then don't take jive off of nobody—not a living soul."

But the Party was in deep trouble. At this very moment, Huey P. Newton, the organization's founder, was probably eating prison fare in the California State Prison near San Luis Obispo, about two hundred and fifty miles beyond San Francisco. He was sent there for fifteen years after being convicted of killing John Frey, an Oakland police officer. Bobby Seale, Newton's first disciple and cofounder of the Black Panthers, was in a San Francisco jail fighting extradition to New Haven, Connecticut. That state wanted to prosecute him for the murder of Black Panther Alex Rackley, who was found murdered in May of 1969. Twenty-one other members of the New York Chapter were buried in New York jails for alleged bombing plots—each under incredible bonds of one hundred thousand dollars. What's more, the police had stepped up their raids on the Panther headquarters and homes.

"We fight the pigs because they have threatened to wipe us out," Hilliard said soberly. "Well, those dudes have to do a lot of wiping because there's a lot of black brothers who feel the same way we do, a lot of them. And they're all tired of getting their asses kicked by racist pigs."

The authorities are hardly secretive about their plans for the Panthers. The police chief of Denver, Colorado, recently told a national television audience that the Panthers "must be dissolved and banished." J. Edgar Hoover, in the fiscal 1969 FBI report, wrote: "Of all the violence-prone black extremist groups, the Black Panther Party is without question the greatest threat to the internal security of this country." The Black Panthers say the police are practicing genocide on black people. The police, through their actions in the ghettos, give credence to that claim. The Panthers spout gun rhetoric at the police. The police take that rhetoric at face value. Now, after twenty-eight Panther and four police deaths, both camps are gripped in a paranoiac state of fear—a fear that is spreading into panic and hysteria.

The Panthers live a semicommunal existence. While David Hilliard cooked, others washed clothes and cleaned the second-floor rooms and hallways. Telephones rang continuously. D.C., as Donald Cox is called, usually answered. Teen-age girls kept several typewriters going at a fast clip. Stencil machines cranked out propaganda sheets and orders to other chapters. The quiet chatter and the noise from the machines gave a businesslike atmosphere to the otherwise dreary floor. The first-floor office, which I had seen earlier, was wood-paneled, orderly and spanking clean. Huge posters of Panther leaders and Panther martyrs, and of third-world heroes such as Mao Tse-Tung, Che Guevara, and Ho Chin Minh covered the walls and street windows. A large portrait of Malcolm X graced one wall. Overlooking it all from a commanding position was a huge poster of Huey Newton, sitting defiantly in a thronelike wicker chair—rifle in one hand, a spear in the other. A FREE HUEY poster still hung over the inner doorway, a throwback to those angry days when Newton was on trial in Oakland's heavily guarded Alameda County Courthouse, fighting a first degree murder verdict and the gas chamber.

As the aroma of rabbit stew filled the headquarters, the

kitchen began filling up. Panthers came from the front and back of the building, from the basement and the street. A bearded young man in Army surplus fatigues came in with four bottles of cheap wine. He popped the corks and set out some glasses. Then everyone went for the stew. David dished me a plate. A little salty, a little tough, but not the moment to complain about the culinary efforts of the Black Panther's chief of staff.

The phone rang. D.C. answered, listened, then summoned David. "The pigs are giving a brother some trouble." David stepped to the phone, mumbled some questions. He listened again then ordered the brother to "sit tight." He nodded to June and D.C. and they began eating faster. Something told me that they were about to move out. I wanted to go with them, so I ate faster too.

These were a lot of mouths to feed three times a day. I asked Hilliard if the Panther leaders held outside jobs. "Jobs?" He seemed astounded. "Brother, we've all got great big jobs—keeping all these brothers and sisters alive and protecting the headquarters. We keep a round-the-clock guard. There's not a minute of the night or day that somebody's not watching." Hilliard, June and D.C. finished and started down the stairs. I grabbed my camera and followed them down to the car. David paused when he saw me. "Drop you at your hotel if you like," he said firmly. "On our way to Frisco for some private business." I accepted.

With the odor of rabbit stew clinging to me I made my way through the great lobby of San Francisco's elegant Mark Hopkins Hotel. The sumptuous restaurants, salons and boutiques sharply defined the gap between the Black Panthers' world and that other world they had set out to change. And for a few uncomfortable moments I felt out of place, disloyal, even traitorous. Then the elevator door sprang open and swallowed me, and I was whisked up toward a hive of carpeted floors, soft beds and snow-white sheets. An obviously well-heeled white family of four got on at the mezzanine. The blonde teenage girl wanted to take in the waterfront the next morning. Her older crew-cut brother was nudging his father toward the golf course. "We have plenty of time. We will enjoy it all," the mother said. A thought crossed my mind: How would the four of them like to have rabbit stew tomorrow night with some brothers and sisters over on Shattuck Street? I smiled at the idea. The father smiled back, and I bade them good night and got off at my floor.

For the next three hours I tossed in my bed, thinking back to the Panther headquarters, and to the whereabouts of the three leaders who had gone off to try and outsmart the "pigs." As I was dozing off it suddenly came to me that I might never see the three of them alive again. It was a dismal thought but a compelling one. When one traces their party's history such a thought is easy to come by.

The Black Panther symbol first leaped into the civil rights struggle in 1965 with Stokeley Carmichael's formation of the Lowndes County Freedom Organization in

Lowndes County, Alabama. It was called the Black
Panther Party because Carmichael wanted to use a
symbol diametrically opposed to the white rooster of the
Alabama Democratic Party. The jungle panther is respected for its savagery in defending itself. It rarely
attacks except for food. Most importantly, it fights off
any animal that challenges its lair. Huey Newton and
Bobby Seale did not form their party as a direct adjunct
to Stokeley's organization, but it blossomed after Huey
had met and talked with Carmichael and discussed the
possibility of expanding to a nationwide political base.

Huey Newton and Bobby Seale had met in the early
1960s on Oakland's Merritt Junior College campus. In-
spired by the Black Panther symbol and buttressed with
a law book and an assortment of guns, they set out to
organize the black young in Oakland who shared their
discontent. There were quite a few around. At a street
gathering one hot night in June, 1966, Huey pointed his
finger in a cop's face and shouted, "We're not waiting
for you to change! We are going to change you!" The
Panthers grew. The police tightened their watch over
them, harassed them, tried to flush them out into open
warfare. Then the Panthers made a bold move. They
began to tail the patrol cars, watching for any police
brutality toward other blacks, whom they would then
advise about taking legal action against their oppressors.
There was one skirmish after another, and several police
ambushes in which some Panthers were killed. When
Eldridge Cleaver got out of prison he fell under Huey

Newton's spell and eventually became the Black Panthers' minister of information. Cleaver, harassed by state authorities, fought back with vitriolic prose. Cleaver and seventeen-year-old Bobby Hutton were ambushed by the police one night. Cleaver was shot in the leg. After the two surrendered, Little Bobby, as the Panthers called him, was shot down and killed. The police say he tried to escape. Cleaver says the cops told the boy to run to the patrol car and when he did they mowed him down. Berkeley became a frightened city. The entire Bay area was saturated with anger and hate between the warring factions.

Despite all this, the posture of the Black Panther Party remained one of self-defense. It was inevitable that the Panthers, in the beginning, would adopt the Muslim emphasis on black dignity and its antiwhite sentiments. As the Panthers grew they went through one crisis of identity after another. The one thing that has remained consistent is the ten-point program drawn up by Newton and Seale in October, 1966, when the Party was founded. The ten points, which are followed by amplifying paragraphs not quoted in full here, are:

1. *We want freedom. We want power to determine the destiny of our Black Community.* . . .

2. *We want full employment for our people.* . . .

3. *We want an end to the robbery by the white man of our Black Community.* . . . The Germans are now aiding the Jews in Israel for the genocide of the Jewish people. The Germans murdered six million Jews. The American racist

has taken part in the slaughter of over fifty million black people; therefore, we feel that this is a modest demand that we make.

4. *We want decent housing, fit for shelter of human beings.* . . .

5. *We want education for our people that exposes the true nature of this decadent American society. We want education that teaches us our true history and our role in the present-day society.* . . .

6. *We want all black men to be exempt from military service.* We believe that Black people should not be forced to fight in the military service to defend a racist government that does not protect us. We will not fight and kill other people of color in the world who, like black people, are being victimized by the white racist government of America. . . .

7. *We want an immediate end to POLICE BRUTALITY and MURDER of black people.* We believe we can end police brutality in our black community by organizing black self-defense groups that are dedicated to defending our black community from racist police oppression and brutality. The Second Amendment to the Constitution of the United States gives a right to bear arms. We therefore believe that all black people should arm themselves for self-defense.

8. *We want freedom for all black men held in federal, state, county and city prisons and jails.* . . . because they have not received a fair and impartial trial.

9. *We want all black people when brought to trial to be tried in court by a jury of their peer group or people from their black communities, as defined by the Constitution of the United States.* . . . A peer is a person from a similar economic, social, religious, geographical, environmental,

historical and racial background. To do this the court will be forced to select a jury from the black community from which the black defendant came. . . .

10. *We want land, bread, housing, education, clothing, justice and peace. And as our major political objective, a United Nations-supervised plebiscite to be held through the black colony in which only black colonial subjects will be allowed to participate, for the purpose of determining the will of black people as to their national destiny.*

The ten points conclude by quoting from the Declaration of Independence:

When, in the course of human events, it becomes necessary for one people to dissolve the political bands which have connected them with another, and to assume, among the powers of the earth, the separate and equal station to which the laws of nature and nature's God entitle them, a decent respect to the opinions of mankind requires that they should declare the causes which impel them to the separation.

We hold these truths to be self evident, that all men are created equal; that they are endowed by their Creator with certain unalienable rights; that among these are life, liberty, and the pursuit of happiness. *That, to secure these rights, governments are instituted among men, deriving their just powers from the consent of the governed; that, whenever any form of government becomes destructive of these ends, it is the right of the people to alter or to abolish it, and to institute a new government, laying its foundation on such principles, and organizing its powers in such form, as to them shall seem most likely to effect their safety and happiness.* Prudence, indeed, will dictate that governments long established should not be changed for light and transient causes; and, accordingly, all experience hath shown, that mankind are more disposed to suffer, while evils are sufferable, than to right themselves by abolishing the forms to which they are accustomed. *But, when a long train of abuses and usurpations, pursuing invariably the same object, evinces a design to reduce them under absolute despotism, it is their right, it is their duty, to throw off such government, and to provide new guards for their future security.*

The Panthers first grabbed national attention when thirty of them—six women and twenty-four men—dressed in black leather jackets and black berets, marched on the California State Capitol in Sacramento on May 2, 1967. Armed with .45s, 375 Magnums, shotguns and rifles, and draped in bandoliers, they walked up the steps of the Capitol building, and Bobby Seale read a statement by Newton protesting a bill then under debate making the carrying of firearms illegal. The bill was passed, but the Panthers were on their way. Against a background of summer riots and the growth of paramilitary groups all over the country, many whites suddenly found the Panther image a frightening and intimidating one. On the other hand, to a multitude of black boys in the ghettos the Panthers were "bad-ass mother-fuckers"—high praise indeed.

In the early days, Newton introduced his "vanguard party" to Marxist and Maoist political theories through mandatory political classes at the Berkeley headquarters. Such teaching, it was explained, gave the Panthers "a chance to be objective in their appraisal of the plight of the black people." At times this has hùrt them more than it has helped. Most hungry black people in ghettos had never heard of Marx or Chairman Mao—and could not care less about them or their theories. They more easily understood angry black people who rebel simply because they were tired of being slammed against a brick wall every night and frisked.

The Panthers, like the Muslims, attract young blacks with criminal records, and for the same reason they have succeeded, to a certain extent, in rehabilitating former convicts. This is not only a source of irritation to the police but aids them in their efforts to stereotype all Panthers as a "bunch of thugs." It has been easy for the police to blame an unsolved crime on the Panthers. And when it boils down to taking the word of either an ex-convict or the police, one knows very well where the odds lie.

On October 27, 1967, Huey Newton and a friend, Gene McKinney, were driving to an after-hours joint. They had reached West Oakland's ghetto area when they were ordered to pull over by policeman John Frey.

"Well, well, look who we have here—the great Huey Newton. Let's see your license and registration papers." Huey obliged. Then another squad car roared up. In it was Officer Herbert Heanes. Perhaps no one will ever know exactly what happened next, but Huey got a bullet in the stomach, Heanes got several wounds, Frey was killed and Gene McKinney got away unscathed. On November 13, 1967, Huey was charged with the murder of Frey. After a long and celebrated trial he was convicted, not for first degree murder, as the Oakland cops had wanted, but on a manslaughter verdict which snatched him from death in a gas chamber. It was obvious that the jury was never sure of who shot whom, or whether indeed Huey Newton was even guilty of manslaughter. When all the testimony was finally in, Officer Heanes's official account of the incident was riddled with contradictions. Nevertheless Newton was sent up for fifteen years. The very next night two Oakland cops, miffed by the "soft verdict," got drunk and opened up on the Panther headquarters with a fusillade of rifle and shotgun fire. One accidentally blew a hole in the roof of their squad car with his carbine. They were charged with felonious assault, but in a show of sympathy, two hundred policemen failed to show up for duty the next day. No one was hurt when the two cops shot up the place that night, but the black community got up-tight—got ready to "lay it on." From his cell Newton ordered calm. "Don't risk sacrificing yourselves to the pigs at this time. We'll move when we're ready. We're not ready now." Oakland remained cool.

Newton's arrest in October slowed but did not halt the Party's political development. In fact, the trial promoted a Panther-white alliance when young white leftist students rallied to the Panther call of "Free Huey!" The Panthers hired white attorney Charles Garry, who did better by them than they had probably expected. It was his skillful defense of Newton in the trial, which lasted from July to September, 1968, that saved his life.

After the gun-control law was passed in California the Panthers shed their weapons and bandoliers. Street dress replaced the black leather jacket uniform, being worn now by young blacks all over the big-city ghettos. They were in effect "cooling it."

But the calm didn't last. It couldn't last. Unprovoked raids on Panther headquarters continued in San Diego, Sacramento and Berkeley. The Panthers were shot at and the Panthers shot back. Some were jailed. Some were wounded. Some were killed. The Mayor of Sacramento actually rebuked the police for their "wanton destruction" of food supplies the Panthers had assembled for their Children's Breakfast Program. Ed Cray of the American Civil Liberties Union said the cops not only destroyed the food but "pissed and crapped on the debris to be sure it could not be used again."

In Los Angeles police cars had relentlessly prowled the Panther blocks, breaking up adolescent groups and frisking individuals. On October 20, 1969, a cruising plainclothes car was allegedly "ambushed" by a car full of Black Panthers. Curiously the only person killed in the ambush was a Panther. One cop was slightly wounded. Case closed.

Then in Chicago before dawn on December 4th of the same year, a team of fourteen State's Attorney's cops shot up a Black Panther apartment on Chicago's West side. When the melee ended the Party's Chicago leader, Fred Hampton, and Mark Clark, another Panther, had been gunned to death. Hampton, apparently asleep when the attack came, never got out of his blood-drenched bed. Four other Panthers were wounded by the intense gunfire laid down by the raiders. Armed with a search warrant for "illegal guns," Sgt. Daniel Growth, who led the raid, told a coroner's jury that they had been fired upon when they entered the apartment. But the Panthers' story, gleaned from interviews with the survivors of the fray and supported by intensive ballistics investigation, held that the police burst in without warning and blasted away. Clark allegedly was killed in the first volley. His companions were crouched inside the door where they had gone to try and arouse the sleeping Hampton. Before the authorities closed the building to the public, a steady stream of black and white visitors filed through the Panther apartment. Black-bereted Panther guides pointed out the bullet holes that refuted the police accounts given to the press by State's Attorney Edward V. Hanrahan. "Here's where chairman Fred was murdered," one said, motioning to the bloody mattress. There were also young white volunteers scattered throughout the place, measuring distances, photographing the bullet-scarred walls, counting the holes.

About a week after the shooting the *Chicago Tribune* came out with a set of misleading and mislabeled pictures, given to them by Hanrahan. He had given the *Tribune* its spectacular exclusive because it "gave an accurate, fair, and balanced account of the events that occurred at the shooting." He had lashed out at other local media for "outrageous publicity" and an "orgy of sensationalism." His police had told of a shotgun blast ripping through the door at them; of furious exchanges of gunfire; of repeated orders to surrender, which the Panthers ignored. The battle, they claimed, raged through the hallway, the bedrooms, kitchen and dining room. Only one detective reported firing a shot into the rear bedroom, from which there was said to have come heavy Panther gunfire. But, when a detective entered the room, he found Hampton lying in the bloody bed, a pistol and shotgun nearby.

In spite of all this Panther gunfire, only one cop was nicked in the leg, through "the grace of God," said Hanrahan. One photograph showed the front door with a hole that was made, said Hanrahan, by a 12-gauge shotgun slug. And there was a close-up of what was said to be the bathroom door opposite the door of the first bedroom. The caption read, "Hail of lead tore through bathroom door in fire from opposite bedroom." A third photograph showed the back door, in the kitchen. Circled were two holes in the doorjamb, supposedly from Panther shots within the apartment.

These pictures, the first evidence offered as proof that the Panthers had fired at the police, drew a howl of protest from newsmen and others who had toured the apartment. No one could recall any holes in the bathroom door or kitchen. No one remembered any marks in the hallway from a shotgun blast. Reporters who hurried back for a recheck found that bullet holes in the kitchen doorjamb were rusty nailheads. The bathroom door turned out to be the bullet-riddled front bedroom door. And there was no sign of any 12-gauge shotgun shell having penetrated the door from inside the living room. Closely questioned about the picture "evidence" at a news conference the following day, Hanrahan explained, "I have made no evaluation of the pictures other than to say that they portrayed the scene accurately." Asked if he was responsible for the captions or the descriptive material in the *Tribune*, Hanrahan replied, "No, we are not the editors." He did, however, concede that the pictures might be in error. And although the paper's editors gave assurance that the captions for the pictures came from the police, Hanrahan in effect had left them holding the bag.

Later Sergeant Growth was questioned by a special deputy coroner during the inquest: "Did you consider the use of tear gas for the raid?" he was asked.

"No, sir, I didn't see any need for it. I was going to execute a search warrant," he answered.

Growth was asked why he considered the raid dangerous enough to require extra weapons.

"The very fact that they were alleged to be Panther[s]. . . . They were known to shoot a police officer, sir."

Why, the coroner persisted, had they not brought tear gas along to avoid the possibility of gun play?

"There was . . . " Growth said, haltingly, "no tear gas available."

Then one dawn in mid-December, 1969, the cops

mounted a "frontal mission" on the Los Angeles Panthers' Central Avenue headquarters. They hurled everything in their armory at the two-story brick building, from high-velocity bullets to shotgun blasts, tear-gas grenades and satchel bombs. The Panthers returned the fire. How the building stood after the onslaught is a miracle. All the windows were blasted out and great chunks of bricks were ripped away. All the window posters were riddled with buckshot. Only one sign was left intact. It read: *Free Huey. Feed hungry children.* The shootout lasted from 5:35 A.M. until five minutes past ten—about four hours and forty-five minutes. By the time the last clouds of tear gas and smoke had cleared, thirteen Panthers, including two women, had come stumbling out of the bullet-riddled building. The two women and six men were wounded. Three cops were also wounded during the opening volleys.

And so the Panther history went. I finally dozed off to sleep in the Mark Hopkins with my mind drowning in it. Neither the Hilliard brothers nor D.C. had returned to the Berkeley headquarters when I reached there the next morning. No one knew where they were—or perhaps they just weren't telling. Calvin, a well-constructed Panther with a neatly cropped Afro, was acting as officer of the day. He sat behind a desk coolly issuing orders to Party members who drifted in for assignments. A white workman came in with a spraying apparatus. "Somebody called about some bugs you've got here," he explained. Calvin stepped over to him and asked him to raise his arms, then frisked him for weapons. "He's clean," Calvin mumbled to another Panther. "Just keep an eye on his spraying." A tall white girl in hippie trappings sauntered down the stairs. Calvin turned on her. "Where'd you come from? Who let you in? Anyone frisk you up there?"

"Nope," the girl answered nonchalantly.

"Stand where you are," Calvin snapped. He summoned a sister from upstairs to do the frisking, meanwhile chewing her out for "gross negligence." "Don't let this happen again," he warned. "This chick could be a dope-drop for the pigs."

I spent the rest of the morning waiting and hoping to get word about Hilliard and the others. None came, but the calm at headquarters seemed a sure sign that nothing serious had happened to them. Around noon I called Charles Garry's office, thinking they might be with him. But he was waiting too. Hilliard, he explained, was to have met with him at ten that morning. It seemed to me now that Garry's office would be the best place to catch up with the three men. So I caught a ride with Harold Holmes, a young Panther Calvin was sending to San Francisco on a Party errand.

Harold was short and boyishly thin, wrapped in an eloquent and chilly indifference. Most Panthers are very tight-lipped with strangers. Harold was no exception. Aside from a grunt or two, we drove for the first ten min-

utes in absolute silence. Then I casually mentioned something about meeting Eldridge Cleaver in Algiers and he
opened up. I found out then that he had joined the
Party about six months before; that he had studied at
Dilliard University and Texas Southern. His Southern
accent, steel-rimmed spectacles, bushy Afro and studious
demeanor were a paradoxical mixture of the Ivy League
and the ghetto. His aims, needs and reasoning were
thoroughly locked into the jargon of third-world philosophy. "Chairman Mao says you fight-fail-fight-fail-fight
until victory is ultimately won. . . . Our Party has already
implemented concrete revolutionary Marxist-Leninist principles to make our people a strong political organ in
themselves. . . . The interest of the local proletariat should
be subordinate to the interest of the world proletariat."
It was strange to be riding beside this intense black boy
who mumbled these controversial theories as if he were
reciting homework. I wondered about this college-trained
young man and several others I had met inside the Party.
I asked Harold what had attracted him to the Panthers.
But by then we had arrived at Garry's office. Harold
wasn't talking any more. "Right on," he said as I got
out. "Power to the people."

Mrs. Dorothy Wood, a handsome middle-class black
woman employed by Garry's law partner, partially answered the question. We had talked in the lawyer's outer
office while I waited for Hilliard to show up. Her son
James, she told me, came home one night and informed
her that he had quit school and joined the Black Panther

Party. "I was pretty upset. At first I thought that he was just infatuated with their black jackets and berets. But very soon I realized he was more seriously involved. After he explained about their breakfast programs for the poor kids and some of their other aims it was easier for me to accept. For the first time he seemed to be genuinely happy to be doing something with his life. Naturally I am worried for his safety. He's been arrested three times, just for selling the Panther newspaper. It's just a type of police intimidation. They dropped charges against him each time. Next week it will probably be the same." For a moment she was reflecting. "I know James. He won't blow up buildings or shoot white people. Joining just made him feel that he was doing something for his people. His grandmother was furious. She wouldn't speak to him for weeks. Then one day she saw pictures of Bobby Seale bound and gagged in a Chicago court. She went into a rage. And that same day she made a contribution to the Party."

Recently Dorothy Wood has been going to the Panther headquarters to help out with office work and the newspaper. "In that way I can also see what my son is doing. I'm not a revolutionary type and I still don't fully understand. But I'm trying. James tries to keep me informed about their goals. Our closeness helps fill what would otherwise be a large gap."

Finally at four o'clock Hilliard and D.C. walked into Garry's office. As we grasped thumbs and exchanged the Panther handshake I gathered hope. Just another hour with them would suffice for the questions I wanted answered. But just as suddenly as they had arrived they disappeared behind the door to Garry's inner office. I didn't see them for another two hours—and then only for a second as they dashed out of the office and into the elevator. "Right on, brother. More power to the people." And they were gone.

"Hell," I said under my breath, "it will be much easier to talk with Bobby Seale." He wouldn't be moving around too much, since he was in jail. I asked Garry if he could get an interview with Seale for me. Sympathetic, he called the prison authorities and made the arrangements. Then the two of us drove over to the prison.

Garry is a rather frail, handsome man with a mane of straight white hair. His eyes haunt you with their cool intensity. The Party members call him "the white Panther." He earned this distinction through his tenacious loyalty to them. At each of a series of outer prison gates Garry would nod to the guards as they passed us through. And each nod, I felt, held contempt. "Concentration camps," he muttered once we were inside the main cell block. "Go in any penitentiary in California and you see nothing but black and brown faces—rarely a white one." I looked about casually at the faces peering at us from behind the bars as we walked along. Their color bore out his statement. Only the guards were white. The very atmosphere of the place seemed to gnaw at Garry's insides. Bitterness had taken over his voice. "The government spends a million and a half dollars for a commission to tell us that the reason we have problems in the ghettos is because people in them have lost faith in the system. Can you beat that?" He shook his head. "Not a single judge will read the report. The District Attorney will laugh at it. The police chiefs will say that these men up there in high places are soft on communism." We turned left and entered a gray cubicle to await the arrival of the prisoner.

Shortly after, Seale, in blue faded prison denim and unlaced boots, came in. The two men grasped thumbs as they had done hundreds of times before. Garry introduced me and for a few moments the three of us exchanged the type of amenities people exchange in bars or living rooms. Our time with him would be limited, and Garry had brought along a briefcase full of business papers. I opened up by saying that I had seen his wife Artie and his son Malik the night before. Then I realized that this might have been the wrong thing to say to a man who was parted from his family. But a hint of a smile came to his bearded face. "How are they?" he asked. "Beautiful," I answered. After a moment of awkward silence I asked him how he was being treated. A frown crept over his brow.

"Worse than big-prison treatment. They keep me in a one-man cell. There's no one to talk with. You get cowboy books and funny papers. No decent literature is allowed. It's like they're hoping your brain will rot from apathy." I asked what to him must have been a lot of routine questions, for he gave me what I had come to feel were routine answers—the same ones I got from every Panther

I had talked to. When Garry started fumbling with some papers I cut off my interview by asking him about the Black Panthers' goals. He fingered his beard and leaped to the answer. "Our goals are the same goals that the white man fights for—a decent education for our children, good jobs and good housing for our families. If the government won't do the job then we blacks must do it."

"And how do you intend to do it?"

"Right now we are working toward a large voter registration in black communities so that we can eventually wrest community control from the police. And as you know we have extensive breakfast programs to feed poor kids in black neighborhoods. In fact, we want just about the same things Martin Luther King wanted. It's only our tactics that differ. The time for begging and praying for deliverance is over. The racist power structure answers praying and begging with more repression, more deceit and more hypocrisy." Small beads of sweat popped out on his brow. "There are some street crossings in black neighborhoods that need traffic lights badly. The kids have to run like hell to keep from getting hit. We will get them across safely if it means we have to use guns." He was angry but far from being in the fierce rage that had boiled over in the Chicago courtroom a few months before. I asked him how he felt after the judge had ordered him bound and gagged. "It's hard to describe," he said. "I was furious at the treatment I got there." He was thoughtful for a moment. "My little boy was there that day. He came running down the aisle saying 'I want my

daddy.' Dr. Spock was there too. He advised my wife not to bring the kid again. He was right. I don't think the kid will ever forget that scene."

Garry drove for several blocks in silence after we left the prison. He spoke softly after we had crossed over Market Street, more as if he were talking to himself. "The law as we know it today is irrelevant to the needs of our society. We need change—abrupt change." He half smiled, half grimaced. "You notice I'm not using the word 'revolutionary.' You've got to be careful with that one, you know."

It was dark by the time we reached the Panther headquarters. "What about this gun business? Are they serious?" I asked as I got out of his car.

"A lot of it's rhetoric. But I tell them they have a right to kill in self-defense, or if they are subjected to brutality." A Panther spotted Garry's car from the entrance to the headquarters. "Right on!" he shouted. "Right on!" Garry shouted as he drove off, his fist clenched in the Panther salute. "Right on," I called back. My fist had also started up. For a split second I started to pull it back. Then—what the hell? My arm stiffened firmly into the defiant gesture.

The first thing I remembered when I entered the Panther headquarters that night was the Berkeley police assault plan. I looked down at the wood floor where sixty rounds of solid slugs were to burst through; at the windows that the 00 buckshot would blast out. I thought of the grenade launchers and submachine guns—the walls vomiting plaster under the intense fire. And I looked at the teen-age girls at the typewriters, at little Malik Seale and two other Panther children playing on the floor. *("Assault squad will then proceed upstairs and bring down the wounded and dead.")* I hoped it would never happen.

With such a document on the premises I wondered how they worked with such calm. Their cool was admirable. It seems that to spend each hour of one's life in such a threatened atmosphere is to court insanity. You observe them there at the stenciling machines, filing cabinets and typewriters, dealing with papers full of words menacing to their very existence. After you are around them a few days you eventually understand that they are just doing what they have to do. And you begin to understand that their enemy *is* the police. And you come to realize that if you are part of the silent majority that wants the police to wipe them out, then you too are their enemy. For you, they point out, serve as a reservoir for the policeman's brutality against them.

Black men like all men want freedom. There are no exceptions. I still fail to see why the Panthers embrace Marxist, Leninist or Maoist dogmas. It's like hoisting a red flag over a black revolution. Yet I, like many other blacks, am at the point where white racism is enough to make me fight. But we must *fight*. We have only a few American revolutionists whom we look up to. The give-me-liberty-or-death cry from a black man in this country has so far meant death. Medgar Evers, Martin Luther King and Malcolm X are substantial proof of this. We measure

...us by the society in which we exist. In our discontent we have burned stores and buildings and ransacked them. Our authorities call this rioting. And a riot, it seems, is permissible a couple of times a year—if it's in a black ghetto. And it always is. But the Panthers have dared to use the word "revolution." They want the system destroyed, not repaired, because they have lost faith in the ability of the system to repair itself—and in its will to do so.

The white man has forever enjoyed the fruit, while the black man has patiently served it. Now the black man wants some of the fruit for his table—not all, just a fair share of it. When all black men come to believe, as the Panthers do, that the white man's answer is an irrevocable and unalterable "no," then the revolution will come. "Not like those in China, Russia, Cuba or Africa," Bobby Seale assured me, "just a Yankee Doodle kind of revolution." During that first encounter with the cops, Huey Newton was attempting to show black people that the root of their problem was fear; that the source of the fear lay in the white man's power to destroy him. "Rid yourself of fear and you rid yourself of white oppression."

Self-protection was the premise upon which the Black Panther Party was founded. Black men armed! The very thought of it filled the white heart with paranoia. Even to all those members of those white gun clubs all over America—it was shocking. Black people going around armed! Violence! Yes. It has been a way of life in the big-city ghettos for years. But police brutality, the crowded kitchenettes, the crimes, the never-ending quarrels and vindictiveness against the rich landlords, the unbearable closeness, the winter cold, the summer heat, the deep hunger, all fathered the violence. These and many other things funnel our lives to ruin and death. For protection it is the law we turn to. But the Panthers have grown to look upon the law as their enemy. Through bloody experience they realize that if they are to survive they must protect themselves against the protectors of the law. For them there is no longer a question of whether or not there is a campaign to wipe them out. They say, "Twenty-eight of us have been murdered." And David Hilliard assured me, "None of us want to be Number twenty-nine. Not if we can prevent it."

It is hard to say what will become of the Black Panthers, what with the raids on their offices and the jailing and killing of their leaders. The Panthers say that for every Panther who is destroyed, eight will take his place. There might well be some substance to this boast. The Panthers have provided a model which the black young yearn to emulate; the romantic appeal of their desperate image is irresistible. And there are those who are no longer young—or not even black—who have come to believe that the truth may lie on the Panther side. While many of the letters which poured into Chicago after the Hampton and Clark killings did not support the Panthers' aims, most of them condemned what they believed to be murder by the police. Demands for an investigation came from such men as Whitney Young, Arthur Goldberg and A. Philip

Randolph, and from such institutions as the American Civil Liberties Union, the Illinois division of the N.A.A.C.P., and the Chicago *Daily Defender*. And as for myself—well, all I know is that if I had been there when Fred Hampton shouted, "You can kill a revolutionary but you can't kill a revolution!" and clenched fists shot upward and "Right on!" filled the air, my own black fist would have saluted, and my own voice joined their cry.

Where are the Black Panthers going? America might find it important to assess the distance they have traveled since 1966—and just how far thousands of other black Americans are ready to travel with them. The hard fact is that they have found a response in the black community. They are the new tide. Survival and black pride compel them.

# 9. Papa Rage: A Visit with Eldridge Cleaver

*FEBRUARY, 1970*

One night, just before I left New York to see Eldridge Cleaver in Algiers, a squad car eased alongside me and stopped. Two policemen jumped out. The older one carried a walkie-talkie and the younger one blocked my path and demanded some identification. I was walking briskly from my East Side apartment, late for the theater. Despite the fact that I, like many other black people, experience this type of harassment constantly, I was impatient. When I asked why I had to identify myself, the younger one warned me that he would run me in if I didn't. "I'd prefer that," I said. He copped out, assuring me that things could be worked out there on the street. Then he informed me I was in a wealthy neighborhood where there had been several robberies lately.

"Do I look like a robber to you?"

"All robbers don't go around wearing little black masks," he said.

"And all robbers don't go around wearing black faces," I countered. As I reached for my wallet to prove once again that I wasn't a criminal, his hand inched toward his gun.

"You two are pretty jumpy," I said, pulling out my card.

I have always tuned out at the term "pig." But when those two fat faces reddened at the sight of that card, I too got the image—very clearly. I turned and walked off.

"Sorry, Mr. Parks." I kept walking. "Just doing our job. Trying to protect you. Merry Christmas." I went on without answering, shocked at my thoughts of rifles with silencers, of rooftops—and pigs.

Several days later I told Cleaver about my experience. He smiled easily and spoke softly. "Things haven't changed much back in Babylon since I've been on vacation." To him my incident must have seemed like absolutely nothing. His last encounter with the California police ended with seventeen-year-old Bobby Hutton shot to death, one Black Panther and two policemen injured, and Cleaver being hustled off to jail with a bullet-shattered leg.

Cleaver was now living with his wife Kathleen and their five-month-old son, Maceo, outside of Algiers in one of those yellowish-white concrete houses that line the Mediterranean coast. It was wet, windy and unusually cold for Algiers. He was slumped in a chair, his legs stretched out, the infant slung across his shoulder. He gently massaged the boy's back. In the soft, rain-filtered light from the sea, he looked like any other father trying to burp his child. But his mind was on a tragic, more violent thing—the killing of his fellow Panthers, Fred Hampton and Mark Clark, by Chicago police. "It was cold-blooded murder," he said in a low voice.

I handed him some clippings from the American press, most of which, I felt, condemned the police action in the killings. Cleaver started to read and I watched for some type of reaction. As his eyes moved over the print his dark face was immobile. Maceo finally burped. Eldridge called Kathleen. "Come get this Panther." As she took Maceo away, Eldridge frowned. "That little cat will give them hell one of these days." He lit a cigarette, took a healthy swallow of Scotch and started reading again. I got up and looked about the house.

There were five rooms, counting a tiled kitchen that also faced the sea. Emory Douglas, the Panthers' minister of culture, and his wife, Judy, occupied one room. Connie Matthews, an attractive girl who represented the Panthers in Scandinavia, had the other room. Off a dark hallway was the "workshop," littered with typewriters, mimeograph machines, printing materials, Emory's posters and Party leaflets in several languages. The large living room-bedroom in which I had left Eldridge was the gathering point.

There was very little laughter in that house. Too many brothers were in coffins or prisons. The cold evenings were spent talking of friends, revolution and death, thinking and planning to Otis Redding's blues, to Elaine Brown's protest songs and to the soul-stirrings of Aretha Franklin and James Brown. It was the cluttered, temporary shelter of a black man in exile—where bags stay packed and all precious things are portable.

Cleaver had finished reading the clippings when I returned. "Well, what do you think?" I said.

"Crap. Unadulterated objective crap. So we have to be shot up and murdered in our homes before people become indignant. We have charged the police with ambush and murder over and over again. Now, after twenty-eight murders, people are taking a look. What are we supposed to do, pray for deliverance?" He asked the question in a soft, dispassionate voice, then answered it himself. "Their deaths will have to be avenged. The cops who murdered them must be punished in the same way they committed the crime."

"Right on, Papa Rage," Kathleen snapped. Her blue-green eyes were smoldering beneath a great copper-colored bushy Afro. Her face, pale, strong and intense, revealed a fearlessness equal to her husband's. "Right on," she repeated. Maceo began to cry. Eldridge picked him up. "He's angry. He was born angry—like a real Panther."

When Maceo quieted, I mentioned that Arthur Goldberg and Roy Wilkins were forming a committee to do some investigating of their own.

"And what are those dudes going to investigate?"

"The killing of Hampton and Clark."

Eldridge scratched his beard and smiled for the first time. "And they will wind up saying the police were justified in shooting the brothers."

"They might find just the opposite."

"It doesn't make much difference what they find. It's too late for their concern. The brothers are dead. All that is left is the problem. The Panther is the solution."

"You know about the great sympathy that has sprung up among even the black moderates since the Chicago incident?"

"Sympathy won't stop bullets. And we can't defend every black person in Babylon. Right now it's a big job just to keep ourselves alive. It's the brother's job, and right, to defend his own home. And there's only one way for him to do that. When cops bust through your door, put a gun in their faces and say, 'Split, mother!' There's alternatives. Call the U.N., or the civil liberty boys, or the police station, and tell them you're being shot up. Then wait."

"What do the Panthers have to offer black moderates other than violence, or a fight to death?"

"Nothing. Not even condolences, for they will bring about their own deaths through their own apathy." He got up and moved across the room. He is big, well over six feet, broad-shouldered and powerfully built. He moves with the brutal grace of a fighter. "Violence? Our people are programmed into worse violence by Uncle Sam. Tell me, why should black boys have to go fight Koreans and Vietnamese boys, instead of the Maddoxes, Reagans and Wallaces at home? A white lunatic can attack a black man on the street. But when the cops come they first club the 'violent nigger.' Violence? We hate it. But is it violent to shoot a cop who breaks into your home bent on killing you? If so, the Panthers are violent."

I remembered that right after the murder of Martin Luther King, Black Panthers spread through the ghettos cautioning angry young blacks against violence and rioting. It only gives the cops a chance to kill more of us, they warned. And I thought it significant that after a study of violence, the Lemberg Center at Brandeis University reported that "of 381 racial disorders occurring between January and August 1969, only 17 involved Black Panthers and of those 17 only eight were violent confrontations between police and Black Panthers."

But the police have demanded the Panthers' heads, and the Panthers pridefully tell the police to come and get them. As I sat there with Cleaver, I thought that to avoid the even greater tragedy, all of us would have to become more than idle witnesses. The police must be urged not to provoke the black revolution into a ferocious blindness; the Panthers must realize that they have emerged as a vital part of our fight, but that reason, more than tough rhetoric, is the order of those thousands, black or white, who would support us. Surely, I thought, somewhere in our history of hatred and death for one another, there must be an even greater place for courage and love.

"What is the future of the young black man in America?" I said.

"Right now their future is in the hands of the Wallaces, Agnews, Nixons, Reagans, McClellans and their cops. The black youths in Babylon won't have a future unless they have the guts to fight for it."

So many times during his own life, I thought, Cleaver has appeared to have had no future. He had found himself while behind prison walls. There he wrote *Soul on Ice*, a powerful and remarkably frank insight into himself. He had been in and out of jail since he was sixteen, and when he left prison, at thirty-one, he got involved in the black revolution, politics and the Black Panther Party.

"And from then on," he said, "the parole authorities gave me more trouble than they did when I was a robber. The cops tried to kill me one night in a planned ambush. They murdered little Bobby Hutton instead. They slammed me into Vacaville with a shot-up leg and revoked my parole without a hearing."

I was in California when Superior Court Judge Raymond J. Sherwin freed him on a writ of habeas corpus, observing that Cleaver had been a model parolee. I told Cleaver that I was surprised at this ruling—since the authorities from Reagan on down had lined up against him.

"That didn't stop them," he went on. "They trumped up some more charges and ordered me back to prison. I knew that if I went back to prison I would be killed. So I split." Now, despite suggestions that, for his own safety, he prolong his "vacation from Babylon," Cleaver told me, "I'm going back home to San Francisco. Two-seven-seven-seven Pine is my address. Nobody is going to keep me away from it."

I asked him if he couldn't do the party more good by writing from Algiers, citing as an example the tremendous sale of his books back in the States. He bristled. "You can't fight pigs with eloquence. I've got to physically commit myself."

If he comes back, and I am sure he will, I believe it is to avoid another kind of death. The death inside him in exile is as bad as the other kind of death I fear awaits him back here. Cleaver is armored with the brutal truth of Panther history, of hard streets and tough prisons. Yet a basic naïveté makes him vulnerable at times. "Do you think Reagan and his cops really want me back?" he asked me with all seriousness. "Or do you think they would sleep better if I stayed lost?"

I didn't know. "But do you want them to sleep better?" I asked.

"I want them in a constant state of nightmare," he answered. He sat down, lit another cigarette and crossed his legs. Then, eying me closely, he told me that the Black Panthers would like for me to join their party. "You could serve as a minister of information." I spent an uncomfortable moment thinking that one over. "A lot of young cats would be glad to follow you in."

"I'm honored," I finally said, "but—"

"We need you more than the Establishment does."

"I'm honored," I repeated, "but you must realize that as a journalist I'd lose objectivity." Objectivity, I thought, the word he hated so much. "I have things I want to report to as big an audience as possible."

"I'm more concerned about young strong cats following you into the Party." He had me thinking—back to the inflexible Malcolm X. Cleaver was proving to be even more intransigent—the most uncompromising individual I ever met.

I explained that my interests go beyond those of the Black Panthers, to other minorities and factions of the black movement who want change. He eased off, suggesting that we leave it open. I wondered whether he felt my position was a creditable one. Looking back to that moment I find that I am displeased with my answer. I should have said: Both of us are caught up in the truth of the black man's ordeal. Both of us are possessed by that truth which we define through separate experience. How we choose to act it out is the only difference. You recognize my scars and I acknowledge yours. You are thirty-five. I am fifty-seven. We meet over a deep chasm of time, the events of which forged different weapons for us. If I were twenty years old now I would probably be a Black Panther. I remember as a kid I always took the first lick before I fought back. But a fist is not a bullet. I too would shoot a cop, or anyone else, who forced his way into my house to kill me. You are risking everything by going back to challenge a system we both dislike. I will continue to fight also, but on my terms. I prefer to change things without violence—providing violence is not thrust upon me. If this is your position, too, then your weapons and mine are not as irreconcilable as you might think.

Cleaver went on: "Black people are afraid to join a militant group. They're afraid the cops will shoot them. That's just why we made the cops our political target—to prove to the brother that cops are just fat, gristle and blood."

I asked him what chances the Panthers had against the overwhelming police power. "If we worried about the odds, we would be defeated from the start," he said.

It was dusk. Kathleen brought in a bowl of lamb stew. Cleaver reached over and spooned a mouthful, talking all the while. "We won't be alone. A lot of whites relate to the same issues that we do. They're just as up-tight. The Establishment will have to deal with them as well. Enough tear gas and head-whipping will establish the common enemy."

"Do you welcome whites to the fight?"

"Of course. There has to be some interconnection. We hope through some sort of coalition to bring a change for everyone. I just don't believe that most whites will stand by and see a minority wiped out without trying to put a stop to it."

"And the Communists? There are a lot of reports that they are trying to infiltrate your party."

"Black people don't need Communists to teach them about trouble. The jails in Babylon produce more rebels and revolutionaries than the Communists could dream of producing back there. An incredible number of those rebels are black, and their numbers are growing by the hour. We are out to tear down the system not with fire, not with guns—but with solid political and scientific know-how. If it comes to guerrilla warfare, individuals will die. But individual tragedy can't block liberation for the masses."

"And what will you build in the rubble?"

"Social justice. If the blacks took power tomorrow and treated the whites like the whites have treated us for four hundred years, I'd try to crush them too. We promise to replace racism with racial solidarity. There are no better weapons. We are disciplined revolutionaries who hate violence. That's why we aim to stop it at our front and back doors. Then we won't have to worry about our children dying in blood-drenched beds."

That night I left Cleaver on a wet, wind-swept street. It was strange that his last words were about social justice, the kind that is irrespective of a man's color. I thought about other brilliant young black men like Stokely Carmichael, Malcolm X and Martin Luther King, one self-exiled, two long since gunned down. I couldn't help but feel that Cleaver's promise, like their dreams, would go unfulfilled. Social justice, it seems, is much more difficult to come by than martyrdom.

# *Postscript*

This book of essays has dealt with a sprinkling of well-known blacks and with what is, unfortunately for all of us, an average black family. It is a small group, and certainly not a representative one. It contains too many of our brightest and our best—those granted the desire and ability to lead. Yet if I were to match each person in this group with his white counterpart—some leaders, several extremists, a celebrity, and a working man—surely the whites would not have suffered in such a uniform way. Look back and sift the carnage: Malcolm X is dead; Martin Luther King is dead; Stokely Carmichael's great promise has been blighted; Muhammad Ali has been dethroned; Norman Fontenelle is dead; his son Kenneth is dead; Eldridge Cleaver and the Black Panthers live under a constant threat of death.

America is still a racist nation. It has not learned much from the turbulent decade just passed. We black people are still perplexed by the blood we must shed and the deaths we must die—as Americans. Some of us are born to be leaders, some to be followers. Some of us are born with great talents, some with none at all. But what seems to matter far more is that we are born black. That single fact would control our destiny above all others. From the evidence, our destiny is not a happy one; nor is it one that black people will, for long, accept.